A PLENTY 降下阴间

JOANNA GADD

"You, O God, did send a plentiful rain;

You did restore and confirm Your heritage when it languished and was weary."

Psalm 68.9
Amplified Bible

上帝啊, 你降下沛雨, 滋润你干旱的产业 - - 以色列。

诗篇 68.9

Chinese Contemporary Bible (Simplified)

Dedication

This book is dedicated to all my friends in China who opened their hearts to me and made me feel like I had come home.

A PLENTIFUL RAIN
Copyright © 2023 JOANNA GADD

Paperback ISBN: 978-1-915223-27-2

All rights reserved.

No part of this publication may be reproduced, stored in a retrieval system, or transmitted in any form or by any means, electronic, mechanical, photocopying or otherwise, without prior written consent of the publisher except as provided by under United Kingdom copyright law. Short extracts may be used for review purposes with credits given.

MAIN BIBLE TRANSLATION – The Amplified Bible (AMP).
All Scripture quotations, unless otherwise indicated, are taken from the Amplified Bible, Copyright © 2015 by The Lockman Foundation. Used by permission.

OTHER TRANSLATIONS
Scripture taken from the New King James Version®. Copyright © 1982 by Thomas Nelson. Used by permission. All rights reserved.

The Holy Bible, English Standard Version (ESV) is adapted from the Revised Standard Version of the Bible, copyright Division of Christian Education of the National Council of the Churches of Christ in the U.S.A. All rights reserved.

Scripture taken from The Voice™. Copyright © 2008 by Ecclesia Bible Society. Used by permission. All rights reserved.

Published by

Maurice Wylie Media
Inspirational Christian Publisher

For more information visit:
www.MauriceWylieMedia.com

Publisher's statement: Throughout this book the love for our God is such that whenever we refer to Him we honour with capitals. On the other hand, when referring to the devil, we refuse to acknowledge him with any honour to the point of violating grammatical rule and withholding capitalisation.

Contents

Introduction	Life Springs from Sorrow 生命在悲痛中萌发	9
Chapter 1	Journey to the East 东游记	11
Chapter 2	It's Raining! 下雨了	19
Chapter 3	Have you Eaten? 你吃了吗	23
Chapter 4	The Lonely Child's Courtyard 孤儿院	29
Chapter 5	Teaching in a Chinese University 在中国的大学教书	35
Chapter 6	The Countryside 农村	43
Chapter 7	This really is China! 这就是中国！	53
Chapter 8	Straight Ahead Bravely 勇往直前	61
Chapter 9	A Sensitive Soul 一个敏感的灵魂	69
Chapter 10	A Glimpse 一瞥见	73
Chapter 11	Learning to Speak 学习说话	79

Chapter 12	Weeping in a BMW 自在宝马车里哭	85
Chapter 13	Double Happiness 囍	93
Chapter 14	Small Stones 小小的石头	99
Chapter 15	Of Loss 丢去的	105
Chapter 16	Beyond Myself 超越老我	111
Chapter 17	Deep Roots in the Desert 沙漠之根	117
Chapter 18	Return 归来	123
Chapter 19	Yin and Yang: At a Chinese Hospital 阴阳: 在中医药院	131
Chapter 20	The Chinese Landlord 中国的房东	141
Chapter 21	Wu Shi Ren Fei 物是人非	147
Chapter 22	The Ordinary Road 平凡之路	151
Chapter 23	A Plentiful Rain 降下沛雨	155
Contact		159

Introduction

Life Springs from Sorrow

生命在悲痛中萌发

There is a garden in an old city in the centre of China in which there is a stone engraved with words from the ancient Chinese. Part of it reads, '*Heaven, when about to confer a great trust upon any man, first exercises his mind with suffering, and his senses and bones with toil… When men are distressed in mind and perplexed in their thoughts, they are aroused to vigorous reformation… From these things we see how life springs from sorrow and calamity.*'[1] These are the words of Mencius, a sage, and 'Heaven' in ancient Chinese referred to a God who was unknown. Yet they are words that nonetheless hold truth, echoes of a greater truth in the Word of God that all the hard things that happen in the lives of the children of God are ultimately for their good, both now and for eternity.

We are all called at some point to walk through the hard stuff. This short book is an account of both a deeply enriching journey to the other side of the world, all too fleeting, and a longer journey through things that were experienced as traumatic and deeply painful. The ancient Chinese sage believed there was a power evident when people vulnerably expressed their innermost thoughts and the truth of their tales. Now, in our modern world, we don't just believe; but we know scientifically that telling our stories truthfully connects us, develops trust, and even changes our physiology. When we find words and utter what was

---

1 http://nothingistic.org/library/mencius/mencius48.html

previously kept hidden and secret within, and when we share the most difficult parts of our stories with other human beings, we come closer to healing. If life springs from sorrow, it is words that give us wings to fly upward and out.

> 'Give sorrow words; the grief that does not speak knits up the o'er wrought heart and bids it break.'[2]

---

[2] William Shakespeare, Macbeth.

CHAPTER 1

Journey to the East
东游记

Beginnings 开始

Sometimes it feels like my life never really began until I went to China. I was twenty-three years old, setting off on an adventure, slightly nervous but full of expectancy. I was like a bird flying for the first time — swinging out into the unknown, leaving behind all those old and familiar things. And below, great vistas opened up. Coming into Beijing on the plane, I saw yellow land and grey mountains, like knuckles protruding out of the earth, bald and knobbly. Stepping off the plane, I smelt China for the very first time — a smell I can't quite describe but is so distinct — perhaps the smell of dusty heat and plastic mats, of cooked shrimp, pungent sesame oil, and the weighty smell of a long, dense history.

In Bournemouth, a few months before I left for China, I lay awake in a strange bed, suddenly aware of the hugeness of leaving home and country for a foreign land I'd never been to before and a people that were still quite strange to me. A Chinese girl at a conference half a year earlier, in answer to my uncertainties, said my smile would see me through. *"How could they not love your smile?"* I came to love that Chinese simplicity — almost childlikeness. In Bournemouth, I dreamt of a photograph. It was full of children's faces, still, frozen in time. They were all Chinese.

My Childhood 我的童年

I wanted to be a missionary when I was a child. I imagined going to Africa because I didn't know anywhere else that missionaries went, and I imagined working in an orphanage because that's what missionaries did — well, the women. In my mind, I lived on a plantation in the middle of the bush. I saw myself standing on my wooden veranda, carrying a black baby, with several other young children holding onto my skirt. Maybe a plane hummed overhead, or perhaps a war was going on. I always had an overactive imagination. I wanted to be a missionary even before I knew what it meant to be a Christian.

I spent most of my childhood in my head. I was a timid and highly sensitive child who wanted desperately to be seen but didn't know how to make myself visible. My dad was an evangelist, and we spent a good deal of my childhood arriving early at countryside chapels where he was speaking and having to wait for elderly men to arrive to open the heavy wooden doors. These men, with their hair as white as an old prophet's, wearing their Sunday suits and their starched shirts, seemed even then to have stepped out of a bygone age. My childhood smelt like polished church pews in summer and gas cylinder heaters in winter — the ones that make your vision blur and your head feel heavy. It hummed with the sound of a fly that echoed in the high ceiling space above us as me and my siblings swung our legs restlessly during another long sermon, wanting to be outside and playing in the long grass yet to be cut among the gravestones.

Later, I would come to love countryside chapels with their worn and tattered hymn books that smelt like old books ought to, the stillness of wood and stone, steadfast and safe, and the token Christian farmer whose warm, coarse hands would gently clasp my small ones on the way out.

I discovered China in Switzerland. We were near the mountains in a hostel. It was warm, and we played in the river, ate barbecued sausages in the evening, and went out on a boat on the bluest lake I'd ever seen. One day, it must have rained, or perhaps it was a Sunday, so we stayed inside. The windows were wide open to the scent of mountains and trees, and we watched a film called *The Inn of the Sixth Happiness*. It told the story of Gladys Aylward, who went to China on a train full of Russian soldiers all by herself and ended up telling Bible stories to dishevelled muleteers as they drank hot tea in her inn. I was twelve years old, and China somehow became lodged in my heart.

In some ways, China had never seemed very far away. My siblings used to laugh at me when I was little because they thought my round face looked Chinese. When my little brother was very small, he called me '*Na Na*' because he couldn't say my name. Years later, in China, friends called me by this name again. For many years, I was jealous of my sister because she had two Chinese friends. Both were daughters of families who owned takeaways in the small town we grew up in. My sister would stay overnight in their homes and come back full of stories about how they lived and the odd things they did — how they slept on mattresses on the floor and ate rice for breakfast as well as dinner! One day, my sister was ill and had to stay at home, so at lunchtime, one of the Chinese girls asked to play with me. We played a jumping game on the school steps. Secretly, I hoped my sister would be ill for a lot longer so I could play with the Chinese girl every lunchtime. Unfortunately, she made a speedy recovery and came back to school the next day.

I had many treasures when I was a child. I was more attached to my possessions, especially my dolls, than I was to people, and I hoarded many precious objects. My favourite was a small wooden badge painted like a tribal mask. I always assumed it was African, but it was actually a Peking Opera mask. It wasn't tribal; it was oriental. My sister routinely stole this badge from my hoard of precious objects, and I just as regularly retrieved it. That was one of the many disadvantages of sharing a bedroom for sixteen years! When I finally had my ears pierced, aged thirteen, we made a trip to a local market to buy earrings. I chose a silver pair with a Chinese character on them. The character was *du* 肚 'stomach,' a strange character for a piece of jewellery, but somehow quite relevant to what was to happen to me much later in China.

Perhaps the most significant thing in my journey to China was discovering relatives who had been to China as missionaries a long time before the country closed to foreigners in 1949. They were Canadians and were instrumental in my dad's conversion, praying for him for many years and writing letters every birthday and at Christmas. They were the only Christians among his relatives, who were otherwise working-class people from the East End and country folk from a small, uninspiring village called Coxley. There were no Christians on my mum's side.

University 上大学了

I didn't have Chinese friends of my own until I went to university. There I made many. In my last year, two of my Chinese friends attempted to teach me Chinese. Cissie taught me the words for tree *shu* 树 and sky *tian* 天 as we wandered around the grounds of the campus. Cara insisted on writing down characters as we ate pizza and drank coffee in our very own 'Chinese corner.' After two sessions, she gave up, and we went and ate a Chinese buffet instead. I forgot most of what they taught me within an hour.

I didn't often go home during the holidays, preferring to stay on and work, so I got to know some of my Chinese friends very well. They couldn't go home, and if they didn't have money to travel, they were stuck in empty dorms for weeks on end. Cissie would invite me to her silent kitchen and cook Chinese food for me. Once, she boiled the knee of a pig and served it with rice and soggy cabbage. The knee was huge and frozen. She lugged it back proudly from the butchers in a cloth bag. It took hours to cook, steaming up the windows and filling the kitchen with an awful smell of boiling bone. I ate it gingerly, already feeling a little nauseous from the smell. I wondered if Cissie had ever cooked before.

To London 去伦敦

During my time at university, I went to London often, mainly to watch Shakespeare at the Globe theatre. On one visit to London, I went to an open day at the London City Mission. There I picked up a leaflet about their gap year programme, and eight months later, after an interview and a couple of visits, they accepted me onto the programme and placed me in a Chinese church shadowing one of their missionaries.

When I went home for Christmas during that year in London, I almost didn't go back. I was working in two Chinese churches — in seedy Soho and affluent Hammersmith. Within those churches, I was one of only a few white faces, and nothing had quite prepared me for such a sudden immersion into the hazy depths of Chinese culture, with all its complexities and subtleties. I wondered what I was doing there, surrounded by all those Chinese faces. The Chinese leaders weren't quite sure what I was doing there either. I sat in on their leadership meetings and tried to make notes. I arranged and then re-arranged the English noticeboard. I was given my own crisp pile of name cards, which I never gave out.

The hardest thing during my week was lunch with the Chinese students who came to our English lessons. I didn't know how to eat the nameless objects floating on the dishes that flowed incessantly out of the kitchens of pokey little restaurants in Chinatown. I couldn't eat lobster with chopsticks or squid soup with a flat spoon. And the students always paid, which I found difficult to accept, knowing I didn't quite merit the title of honoured teacher — far from it! I was a mere shadow, a tag-along, not quite fitting. (If someone ordered me squid today, I'd cry with joy — even better if they paid!)

As the year wore on, my responsibilities increased, and I established more of an even footing. I started to enjoy teaching English and eventually received my own small class of five that included a rosy-cheeked baby, nicknamed 'Small Fat.' I read the Bible with a Catholic student I met while giving out Christian literature and eating hot crepes at a London university. I taught Bible class to naughty Chinese boys, and every week I visited Smiley, a small lady with brown teeth and tiny eyes that disappeared altogether when she grinned. She sold cheap plastic knick-knacks and 'lucky cats' in Chinatown. Whenever I visited her corner of the indoor market, she always made me sit down on a pink plastic stall and relentlessly tried to persuade me to eat peculiar-looking vegetables in foil tubs. Mr Lim had a stall outside the market, selling lighters with a marijuana leaf design and fake designer sunglasses. We would stand talking to him until it grew dark and he began to pack up. We often visited the people in the Chinese medicine shop. I liked to go there just to look at all the strange things that filled the glass jars behind the counter — dried flowers and slithers of bark, snake skin and golden powders. The shop smelt like thick, dark syrup. I wanted to try an ear candle but never got around to it.

Chinese culture was full of surprises, some more welcomed than others. At a Christian conference, I had to share a bed with a stranger. There were too many Chinese and not enough beds. Somehow, they only realised that when we all got there,[3] but it didn't seem to bother them. I developed a bond with the church caretaker, and one evening he made me dinner. I visibly blanched when I realised I was expected to eat the eyes of the fish, this being a delicacy and the best part of the meal. I wasn't used to eating anything with bones or gristle and was always slightly startled when someone spat something nasty out onto the table, particularly if it happened to roll in front of me.

My flatmate at the time told me that at the beginning of my year in London, I shared with her that I'd really like to go to China and

---

3 This is a common example of both Chinese inefficiency and what a Chinese friend regards as the root of all evils in China – its vast number of people.

work with orphans. I have no memory of that conversation. In those early months, I was drowning in my mini-China and not enjoying the experience very much. If someone had given me a way of escape, I might have taken it. But by April, things were beginning to change. I stopped fighting against becoming a teacher — the job that everyone had insisted I would do ever since I was a child, and I had always been adamant that I would not. More importantly, I was beginning to fall in love with China — not so much the culture at that time, but the people. I felt relaxed when I was with Chinese people and natural, like I could be myself. And there was a feeling much deeper, at the core, a feeling of somehow coming home.

In April, at the conference where there weren't enough beds, a preacher spoke about missions. It was a series of powerful messages. I made a pledge and signed a card that read: *'Today I decide that Jesus Christ is Lord and Master of my life. I no longer want to merely include God in my plans. I want God to include me in His plan, whatever that means, whatever the cost. Anything, anytime, anywhere.'* I arrived back in London, excited but not sure where this would lead. Teaching was something that had opened up to me, and my love of being with international students had narrowed to being particularly interested in the Chinese. My flatmate and I prayed about it. Was it even conceivable to go to China? She sent an email to a mission agency, and we waited. We finished the gap year, and I went home with no plans, but the ball was already rolling, and my year of 'attempting to go to China and failing' was just beginning.

Returning Home 回家了

I needed that year 'stuck' at home in more ways than I could imagine, though at the time I didn't like it. I was itching to go, eagerly awaiting the next adventure, but God was saying to stay awhile. I couldn't get a job for what seemed like ages (actually, it was three months). I tried and failed to teach myself some Chinese. Over the course of seven months, I was given three placements teaching English in China, and one after the other they all fell through. Not knowing what to do, I went to Bournemouth for teacher training, discovering in the process that had I travelled to China with no teaching qualifications or understanding of anything — from how to introduce new vocabulary to the importance of phonetics — I would have completely floundered, and my students' English would not have improved in the slightest. While I was at home, teaching a Bengali boy in a local Indian takeaway, I came across a small Christian organisation. I'd heard their name a year before when a friend who worked with international students said to me: *"If it doesn't work out with that mission agency, try this one instead."* I dismissed what she said. Why would it not work out? Such a strange thing to say! But in April, between teaching my Bengali boy prepositions and reminding him to use full stops, a family friend sent an email suggesting I contact this organisation. It was my last attempt to go to China.

Four months later, in the sweltering heat of August, I stepped off the plane in a large Chinese city, and life really began.

Chapter 2

It's Raining!

下雨了

They lacked rain there in that ancient walled city, in that central province that was as dry as old powdered bones in a medicine shop. It was a thirsty land. You woke up with lips cracked and stuck together, a mouth full of dried heat, with your tongue large and heavy, and hard saliva like a film coating your teeth. In the morning, the glass next to the bed always had a layer of thick yellow dust floating on it. That yellow dust, even with windows closed, invaded the house, usurping the floors, settling onto books and ornaments, and glistening in the air when the sun finally managed to penetrate those filthy clouds and smog.

But it did rain sometimes. The Government made it rain so that the crops could grow, and the people could eat. When they flooded the sky through what is known as cloud seeding, it was *da yu* 大雨 'big rain.' There was nothing small about it, nothing delicate and fine. It rained for days, fat drops falling fast, drowning the pavements, filling cracks and broken slabs so that when you stepped on them, hidden under brown puddles, the dirty water sprayed up your leg, smelling of drains and mud.

Taking the bus was dangerous; the floors were wet and slippery. The buses swerved and thundered along, and alighting was even more of a risk. Sliding towards the exit and stepping off into a lake, only to find that moments later you were splashed by the traffic behind you.

Dodging the multitude of umbrellas could have been a game if there wasn't the very real risk of having your eye poked out by the spokes of an auntie's ancient umbrella. These Chinese aunties were retired ladies and mature housewives who spent their days at vegetable markets and sat on tiny stools gossiping on street corners. They exuded a confidence and self-assurance that I've not seen anywhere else, and they were never afraid to cross-examine or question anyone. Likewise, they were never in the wrong.

On rainy days, no one moved for you. No apologies, no umbrellas lowered and held to one side so that you might pass by without injury. Like taking a bus or hailing a taxi, it was a fight for survival in which only you were on your side.

When it rained, everyone wore plastic ponchos. Through the endless sheets of grey water, bright spots of red, green, blue, and yellow, buzzed by on mopeds and electric bikes like strange insects, brilliant flies. It was like another world when it rained. A world blurred by water. It might have been dreamlike, save for the uncomfortable feeling of soaked feet and the smell of damp refuse that grounded one back in reality.

On a rainy day, after class, I always went to my favourite steamed dumpling restaurant and sat inside instead of taking them away. The windows were steamed up and dripping with condensation. Wiping a hole with my sleeve, I could look out at the people scurrying past. There were older people, aunties and uncles, on their way home for lunch and a nap. Those dumplings were delicious — egg and chive, pork and fennel, lotus root. They arrived, twenty plump dumplings on a scratched white plate, sitting contentedly like little lumps of pale sunshine basking in their own heat. Chopsticks and a bowl of soy sauce followed, and sometimes a bowl of white boiled water from the kettle resting on the stove. Afterwards, I too walked through the complex to my fifth-floor flat, shut the heavy metal door, and lay down, the rain still falling steadily outside, distant now and not so loud.

It always rained in April on *Qing Ming Jie* 清明节. This was Grave Sweeping Day, a celebration for the dead. On the days before the festival, wooden stalls popped up outside the gates of housing complexes and on street corners, selling paper money and paper houses, paper clothes and cars, and mobile phones. Anything one might possibly need or want in the life hereafter. At dusk, in the half-light, dark figures crouched on the ground, searching for a dry 'auspicious' spot to draw a circular grave with chalk, light a fire, and burn their paper provisions for someone long dead or a relative recently departed. At night, small fires flickered across the city. In the days after, the city smelt of burnt paper, and I avoided stepping on those mass graves, darting around the piles of black ashes, until the rain washed all their remains away again.

A friend took me to a real graveyard once, on Grave Sweeping Day. It was way out in the countryside. And it was raining, of course. The graves were on a hillside; thousands of them, all the same: Black stone heads, standing erect and solemn in the misty drizzle. They went on and on as far as the eye could see, finally lost in the dense fog that drifted up from the wet fields below. My friend bought some cake and some candles and placed them by the headstone of her mother-in-law. She lit incense and held the umbrella while her husband knelt uncomfortably before the grave, attempting to bow. He spoke some words. I wandered amongst the graves. There were no flowers here and no trees. There were just cakes getting soggy, piles of wet fruit, and red candles quietly dripping. Curls of incense ascended through the rain, which now fell like feathers.

Kim gave me a book of poems written by a poet from Taiwan. He found it on his mother's bookshelf. In it, I found my favourite poem, *Waiting for You in the Rain*. I tried to translate it, and in doing so, I may have made my own poem. One part reads: *'If you come or don't come, it is the same; every lotus flower resembles you.'* The Tang dynasty poet Li Shangyin wrote a poem called *Xi Yu* 细雨 'fine rain' or 'drizzle'. I like the character *xi* 细. It means *'thin or slender,' 'soft', 'delicate', 'fine.'* The right side of the character is a field, the left side silk. When I think of *xi yu* 细雨 'drizzle,' I think of soft silk falling on fields of rice.

The best thing about the rain was that it cleared the air. In the days after the deluge, we could see the mountains to the south. These reminded me of Gladys Aylward, climbing for days over vast mountains through much difficulty, leading around a hundred orphans to safety. I wondered where those children ended up. Where are they and their children and grandchildren are now, and do they still remember her stories? In turn, my eyes would move from the mountains, as immovable and impenetrable as they were, to the God of the mountains, the God who abides in the highest places and promises to move the mountains of difficulty in our own lives if we put our trust in Him. *"We journeyed through dangers, through fire and flood, but You led us finally to a safe place, a land rich and abundant"* (Psalm 66: 13 VOICE). After it rained, there was always a freshness, a cleanness, a lifting of the smog, and one could remember those things and be inspired once again.

Chapter 3

Have you Eaten?

你吃了吗

My students told me stories of finding worms, maggots, and bugs in their bowls of stir-fried vegetables in the school canteen. Every school canteen was a terrifying place, and at my university, the food was particularly suspect. When I ordered noodles with my British friends Grace and Tom, they arrived wet and limp, tasting of damp flour and old tomatoes. I'd persuaded them to go to the canteen for dinner, instead of traipsing out of the campus and trying to find a restaurant in the dark. Needless to say, we didn't eat very much, and after that, we always ate outside, even if we had to walk several blocks and it was late and we were tired.

The school canteens were huge — four floors with hundreds of plastic tables screwed to the floor. There were several counters on each floor, and behind the counters, huge metal woks lay smouldering over enormous fiery stoves like dormant volcanoes. Violent streaks of congealed oil covered the walls and every lunchtime, the woks erupted into flames, scorching the ceiling black. The students flooded into the canteen as soon as it was twelve o'clock, grabbed some dishes, slurped, swallowed, spat out bones and gristle, and were out of the door within ten minutes for the next student to fill their seat. There was no sound of conversation, just the rhythmic clink of chopsticks on metal. Eating was a necessity, and the best part of lunchtime was spent napping in the dorms.

If the students had some money, they could eat outside. At the Northern campus, a hoard of ramshackle restaurants had sprung up outside the West Gate to help satisfy the insatiable hunger of the (mainly male) students. I met students there for lunch or dinner, and I remember one occasion when a group of us ate with an American teacher. The restaurant was like a cardboard tent, with yellowing walls and flimsy plastic cloths thrown over large round tables. We ordered fried rice with various dishes. With only a few mouthfuls left, the American teacher turned over her rice to discover the corpse of a large beetle buried beneath. She decided rather quickly that it must have fallen from the ceiling onto her plate. Eating outside the campus wasn't much better than eating inside.

In my first two years, I didn't eat very well because I only spoke a little Chinese. I struggled to remember the names of dishes that I liked, so when I was alone and went to a takeaway restaurant, my choices were limited. The supermarket was a long walk from the campus. It was an underground grotto selling live crabs, cucumber-flavoured crisps, and aisles of MSG. I didn't know what to buy, and I couldn't cook what I bought because the only hob in my dorm was designed for fast, furious Chinese stir fries, and the lowest setting burnt everything to cinders. There was no such thing as *'gently simmer,'* although my Chinese dictionary contained a phrase called *wen huo* 文火, meaning *'small flame when cooking and simmering.'* I never saw any small flames in China. At least I had a microwave, kindly donated by someone who was leaving, and a rice cooker that promised to cook eggs as well as rice. It lied. Very soon, I invested in a tiny red oven that could bake one tray of cookies at a time and became responsible for many baking parties over the next four years. These were always long affairs because of the limited size of the oven, but that gave us more time to chat.

So, in those early months, I made a lot of friends. Not only because I needed them, but because I liked to eat, and I was fed up with boiled pasta from the foreign supermarket. A friend tried my macaroni cheese once and said it was like baby food. I said it was American. Chinese people love to eat. For them, eating is a pleasure — a joy. It can take hours around a boiling pot of gleaming soup, cooking one dish of 'see-you-tomorrow mushrooms' at a time, or on the streets, perched on plastic stools, ordering one tray of skewered barbecued lamb at a time. That's how it happens; one dish at a time, everybody dipping in, the lazy Susan spinning round and round, dishes whirling by with chopsticks flashing in the air. We always ordered together because we always shared.

All year round, the streets were heaving with food: cold noodles in the summer, soaked in vinegar and covered with heaps of grated cucumber. They were best eaten from the vendor on the corner, under a parasol, with a glass of orange soda plucked from the polystyrene freezer. *Rou Jia Mo* 肉夹馍, which is a juicy meat, was delicious wedged in flat bread, wrapped in a brown paper bag and dripping all over my fingers. There were all kinds of noodles: over-the-bridge noodles, spinach noodles, rice noodles, noodles as big as your belt, noodles as skinny as a shoelace, flat noodles, round noodles, fried noodles, steamed noodles, noodles doused in hot oil, and noodles swimming in unison in a deep bowl of salty soup. In the mornings, I bought fried dumplings, savoury pancakes, or steamed buns stuffed with spicy pumpkin, tofu, and glass noodles, or pork and Chinese chives. In the winter, there were always toothless old men, as dark as their rusty drum ovens, peddling baked sweet potatoes. In the summer, truckloads of watermelons drove in from the fields, and the best snack going was runny pineapple on a stick.

Fruit was always seasonal. Persimmon, pomegranates and apples were plentiful in the autumn; hawthorn and pomelo in the winter; strawberries in the spring, lychees, grapes, watermelon, and peaches in the summer. You waited for it, and when it came, you knew what the weather would be like and what would follow, and you gorged yourself on that fruit for a whole month and never thought to freeze it. Fruit-picking in the countryside was a day out. We went strawberry picking in the suburbs, to a place where there were hundreds of strawberry farms all along the road. They were manned by round-faced, ruddy-cheeked ladies in straw hats. The strawberries were fat and red and claimed to taste like milk or chocolate. In late summer, Sue took me to a peach orchard. The trees were dense, and the peaches were heavy. The air shimmered and insects buzzed; we were sweaty before we started, and some of the peaches just melted in our hands; they were bursting with so much ripeness. Squatting, Sue and her aunts tore off the skin with their teeth, spitting it out on the grass. They sucked the flesh into their mouths, the juice dribbling down their chins. This is the way to eat peaches, I thought to myself. On our excursions to the countryside, we saw fields of watermelon too — huge green globes exploding out of the earth. And Sue showed me her own crops — her parents' small rows of cabbages, planted vulnerably in the mud.

The reputation of British food — tasteless, colourless, and overcooked — was well-known in China. I told my friends that at home I ate potatoes in one form or another every day. They looked knowingly at each other. *"That's why British people look like potatoes,"* I added. I set out to prove that the worldwide reputation was wrong. I made countless casseroles, soups, pasta dishes and curries for countless different people. Some were a complete disaster. My leek and potato soup with homemade bread was disappointing for two friends. I think they thought they'd missed the main course, as in Northern China, soup is always served at the end of a meal as a 'filler' or to help digest. More often than not, friends compared the dish I made to something similar in China, as if suggesting that nothing British was truly unique. *"We Chinese have been eating this dish for thousands of years!"* My curries reminded them of Hui[4] food; pasta was just noodles in a different shape; and even ice cream was apparently invented for an Emperor who was feeling too hot one summer over a thousand years ago. It eventually made it to Italy along the Silk Road, where it then became world famous. Perhaps there is some truth in that. The only purely British foods that hit the spot were cakes, biscuits, and desserts. Everyone wanted to learn how to bake. They couldn't wait for them to cool and ate brownies and muffins straight out of the oven, burning the tips of their fingers. The girls complained that they were too sweet, and they'd get fat if they ate just one, but within the hour

---

4 A Muslim ethnic minority

not one cake was left on the plate. I was loved because of my cakes, and I was forever baking. It's a wonder my tiny red oven didn't pop its clogs.

Friends liked to cook for me too. Older friends used their own kitchens, but the young students came to mine. They were enthusiastic but extremely messy and used every cup, plate, and dish they could find. The windows were thrown open, and the kitchen filled with smoke. The tiled floor turned black, spotted with squashed aubergine that got stuck to slippers and made it around the flat to far distant corners. They washed everything in tap water before using it: rice, meat, vegetables, plates, cutlery, and dishes. Sometimes I had five or six girls in my box-like kitchen, bossing each other around in Chinese and chopping away at spring onions. When all was done, we ate like queens and afterwards formed a team to clean. Their standard of cleanliness wasn't quite the same as mine, and they always used cold water to wash up. My tea towels bemused them, as in China, wet dishes are put straight back in the cupboard. Cooking parties were always heaps of fun, but you needed half a day to recover from them.

Formal banquets were something else. The English Department's annual banquet began at six pm and was promptly over by eight. Hundreds of dishes were ordered and picked at during those two hours but never wiped clean. Every few minutes, a teacher or professor stood up and made a toast. We all stopped eating and stood up, chairs scraping the floor, to down a shot glass of *bai jiu* 白酒 'white spirit.' We did it so often that it wasn't any wonder that dishes weren't finished and that the male members of the faculty grew red in the face and slurred in their speech. Once, I accompanied a visiting scholar from Germany to a banquet. Afterwards, we all watched him stumbling across the road to his hotel. The Chinese professors were in fits of laughter (and almost as unsteady on their feet). Thankfully, as a female, I got away with not drinking alcohol. At every banquet I attended, I was always seated next to someone whose task it was to help me fill my plate. This was a great honour and a great nuisance. They insisted on picking up the most delicious things and plonking them on my plate. Chinese taste is very different from Western taste, so I often ended up with deep sea monsters instead of a bit of mushroom.

There are lots of horror stories about food in China, concerning food hygiene and food quality. Rumour has it that many street vendors and small restaurants use gutter oil (waste oil collected from such diverse sources as restaurant fryers, grease traps, and sewage). I heard stories of noodles made partly from plastic and restaurants serving old rice leftover from the week before. A British teacher at my university was walking along one day when she was startled by a chef rising up from a manhole in front of her, like a ghostly Chinese apparition, complete in his white apron and hat. He grunted, wiped his hands on his trousers, and went back into a nearby restaurant to finish whatever he was cooking. We always laughed these stories off. Just like we laughed off the fact that most days in winter, the pollution levels were *hazardous* with warnings to *'stay at home'* and *'don't venture out.'* The whole population kept going, so we did too.

Chapter 4

The Lonely Child's Courtyard

孤儿院

The first Welfare Centre[5] I went to was in another city to the south of mine. The journey took hours by bus through a mountain range, through long, dark tunnels, and over great stone bridges into a valley. Nearing the city, the scenery gave way to fields where coolies drove buffalo — that traditional Chinese picture of round straw hats and wooden ploughs — and you knew then that you were *'South.'* The city itself was non-descript, filled with the same grey Soviet-style buildings found everywhere else in China. It was a smaller city with less people and fewer cars. Most people got around on bicycles and mopeds. There was a river too, twisting its way around the city like a huge, lethargic dragon. We went to a museum in the cold rain and to a green lake way out in the countryside the next day, when it was steamy and hot. On the last day, we went to the orphanage. At that time, the children were living in a series of older buildings while workers painted murals of Winnie-the-Pooh on the walls of a new building. The old buildings felt cramped and chaotic; the new one a white, empty shell. We only stayed for a couple of hours. We saw the babies in the nursery. I didn't know how to hold one then. And we watched the older children have a PE lesson in the courtyard, standing awkwardly, unsure of how to act, smiling at them but afraid to touch, afraid to get any closer. What could we offer anyway? The Chinese word for orphanage literally means the

---

5   State orphanages are called welfare centres in China.

lonely child's courtyard. On that day, in that courtyard, I also felt lonely, cut-off and disconnected from these thin children wearing worn out clothes, their large eyes full of hunger. One staff member seemed more interested in having his photo taken with us. When we left, I didn't think I would ever go back and wondered, in a way, why we'd ever gone.

It was my second trip to this city that made the deepest impression. I discovered then how far the orphanage was from the city — not just in distance. No buses went there. You had to arrange a private taxi that drove past the urban sprawl of squat apartment blocks and out past the garages and workshops, turning and following a dirt track road past older wooden buildings that eventually disintegrated into fields. The taxi dropped me off in a small village, outside the Welfare Centre's iron gates. Behind those gates were treasures hidden in the darkness. The old buildings were still there from my first visit, almost three years earlier. Some were abandoned. I walked around them one evening. They were full of dried leaves, and there were drawings of crayoned animals peeling off the walls. The other old buildings, coloured in pale pastel shades, were where the children lived — four or five children with a house mama in each apartment. The new building was the centre piece of the complex. It was like a hospital and contained classrooms, kitchens, a nursery, and clinics. It sat on the playing field, with a tiny playground to one side which had a bright plastic slide and swings that smelt fresh, like they were unwrapped yesterday. Even the grass looked new and unscuffed, without even a footprint. Bunting hung down from the building, pinned to the immaculate grass, with yellow, blue, and green flags that were stationary and still in the warm air. It was always so quiet. There were no sounds of little feet running down the long, white corridors. No sounds of laughter, singing, or chattering. Even Winnie-the-Pooh seemed as cold and remote as a fat golden Buddha laughing down at the world, immune to its sufferings, believing they don't really exist.

These of course are my perceptions, the impressions of an outsider looking in, perhaps not always seeing everything clearly. Yet I was very aware of the unseen spiritual world, the war between good and evil that was being fought in this relatively small institution in an obscure village in the middle of China. In this place I knew there were Chinese brothers and sisters, quietly, obediently pouring out Love Himself into broken hearts and lives, penetrating the shadows with His light, and by His power making inroads into places of confinement, to release and to set free those born into captivity and held by the darkness that covers so many pockets of this world.

I spent a day in the nursery with the little ones and a day in a room with the severely disabled. I helped brush their teeth in the morning and folded their clothes when they came back from the laundry man, whose room sat in a hut on the roof. I held them and sang songs. Most of the children lay on their backs; some were already teenagers. There in that room with those children, I felt the love and presence of God. Later, when I read these words written by a Chinese sister, I was transported back there: *"Is your soul clean? Isn't your heart deformed? Will you take care of My children?" It is very natural to say these children are ugly, smell bad or [are] too disabled. But when hearing the words from God, my heart just melt[s] as I know my soul and heart are much more deformed than these children.'*

In the evenings, when the new building was even emptier than it seemed in the day, I walked down those dark corridors, across the playing field, flags now blowing soundlessly in the night breeze, to visit the house mamas and the children now home, sat on wooden chairs in front of the TV. I saw a child I knew before, Jia Jia whom I used to take swimming when he was in a home for orphaned babies in another city. He had eyes that sparkled and were full of smiles. His body was twisted, and his head was so heavy that he struggled to lift it. He was lovely and funny, and always asking for food. He had what all children have – a hunger for living and a desire for life itself in all its fullness.

Most evenings, when I was alone in my room, a boy knocked on my door. He was probably about twelve years old. I asked him once how long he'd been in the orphanage, and he said he didn't know; he couldn't remember. Perhaps he'd been there forever. He'd sit down, and we'd talk a bit. Eventually, he would ask for food or money. I gave him some biscuits, and he left until the next evening, when his familiar tap would sound on my door again.

At lunchtimes, the staff cycled or drove across twisting roads through endless fields to the Adult Welfare Centre for spicy beef noodles in the staff canteen. I was dismayed to discover they only served one dish, and the chef was shocked to hear that I didn't want any spice in it. This Welfare Centre was even more remote than the children's centre. There wasn't even a village around it. I never saw any of the teenagers or adults that lived there. It was the same in the Adult Welfare Centre (AWC) that sat under a mountain on the outskirts of the city where I lived. There were hundreds of people who lived there, but every time I went, I only saw a handful. I never met the staff; I just glimpsed one or two in dark suits through a window as they disappeared deeper into an inner room.

At the AWC in the city where I lived, it was still in the courtyard where the elderly people napped. They all wore the same grey tracksuit; we saw countless tracksuit bottoms hanging on a line. This was the home of the deaf and the mute, the criminal and the disabled, the mentally disturbed, and the homeless. All living together in one compound. Anita took me there. She went to teach the deaf and dumb to sign and brought music and dance, stories, and crafts to people who would otherwise be left twiddling their thumbs the whole week. I went to see a boy called Lucas, so he would know that I hadn't forgotten him. He'd been sent there from a project in the city. My first visits to most of the orphanages I went to were because children I had known and loved had been sent there.

Every time I went to the AWC, I was suddenly ill. There was an oppressiveness about the place. The first time I went, it was winter, and the snow was melting in the city, but in the AWC it was still cold. On the rickety bus out to the countryside, the sun poured through the windows, and in its heat, I developed a sudden fiery throat. It was with a steaming nose and eyes that I finally stepped off the bus at the foot of a hill, feeling that I had as much strength as a twig. Lucas and I wandered around the frozen grounds, talking. He told me he wasn't planning on staying there long; soon he would be out, going to a school where they'd teach him how to use a computer.

The second time I went was in March. I gave Lucas some Lego and put it together for him to make a boat. In the warm sunshine, we walked around again. Lucas had a nasty gash on his chin. He said someone had struck him. I don't know how true his words were. He was angry at the time — angry with the world. He said that people treated him like nothing. He spoke fast and for a long time, and I struggled to understand it all, guessing at words I didn't know. On the bench, a strange green fly stung my neck, and by the evening it was swollen.

The third time I went, I took my parents. It was summer. The bus felt almost feverish. We visited the bathroom when we arrived, but there was no running water. We sang songs, told stories, and gave testimonies. I can still hear Lucas singing with gusto: *"Hallu hallu hallu hallelujah, praise ye the Lord!"* For some reason, at that time, he seemed smaller than before. That night, not one of us could sleep. The flat felt heavier than just the darkness of the dead of night. We all tossed and turned all night and, in the morning, cancelled our trip to see some old rock carvings in another city. A few days later, Lucas appeared on my doorstep, having escaped from the AWC. He trod dog poo through my flat, before I gave him an apple, not sure of what to do. After some phone calls, I took him to the project he used to be part of. Eventually, I heard Lucas was taken back to the AWC. The runaway found no refuge with me. I was powerless to help him in any concrete way, or at least not in the way he wanted — rescue from a welfare system that had institutionalised him, that had sought to remove him from society and contain him somewhere far away enough from everything else.

Man Man was another child that was sent back from a project to a state Welfare Centre. She was sent back because she was too old for the orphaned babies' home which specialised in looking after the very little.

She was also profoundly disabled and had not been adopted. I went to her Welfare Centre three times. The third time, Janet took me because she used to work there. Janet really wanted to show me the orphanage because it had been such a huge part of her own life. Somehow, we managed to get in, though the gatekeeper was suspicious. Janet's small son went with us, so we spent most of the time on the trampoline outside, bouncing over the broken part. The ponds were all frozen, including the small waterfall that had frozen in mid-flow, and we were the only ones in the grounds. It was late afternoon. Before we left, Janet suggested we go into the building behind us so she could show me the floor where she used to work. *"There's a Chinese sister there,"* she said. *"She will let us in."* We snuck up the stairs, Janet's son running in front. I remember the green netting under the landing and teddy bears on the bannisters. She took me to a higher floor, and I saw rows and rows of beds and cots. In each bed was a teenager with cerebral palsy, and in each cot was a child. Some of the more able children were up and about, going around on wooden chairs with wheels, but most were lying down. In the larger room, aunties were busy changing nappies. They were extremely efficient, taking only a couple of minutes at each bed. Janet gave me a bowl of rice porridge and took me to the smaller room with the cots. There were about fifty children in there. *"Let's help the aunties feed them,"* she said. I went closer to the cots to see the children. Some were crying, others were slowly rolling their heads along their pillows or against the sides of their cots, possibly seeking sensory feedback, and some just lay there staring blankly at the ceiling. I chose one of the cots and started to feed the little boy lying there. The other aunties were already on to their third or fourth child. They didn't sit the children up or even talk to them. My boy was about four. His thumb was swollen and red from where he constantly sucked it. He was fine when I fed him, but when I touched him, he began to cry. Upset, I cried too. When Janet came up, I said, *"This place is horrible."* She was upset by my words. "Years ago," she said, *"things were much worse. Many children didn't make it."* I realised then the extent of the work, the long way they had come, fraught with many challenges, and the long road ahead that was still there to tread. Then Janet cried too, and we left.

Chapter 5
Teaching in a Chinese University
在中国的大学教书

For two years, I lived and worked at a large University. It had many campuses, and I lived on the main campus, on a ring road that was notoriously difficult to catch a taxi, and a good twenty-minute walk over uneven paving stones to the nearest underground station. I lived in the Foreign Experts Building, which was squat and grey and covered in dense green vegetation so that it looked like a secret government building, uprooted from a steamy jungle and dumped next to the school running track. It may not have been full of experts, but it was full of foreigners. And mosquitoes, due to a stagnant pond that lay festering directly outside the building. There were also geckos who lived in the vines and behind my curtains, and large, ugly cockroaches. About six foreign teachers lived quietly in the building; the other residents were students from Kazakhstan and the Congo. They were anything but quiet. The Congolese threw wild parties every weekend in the downstairs foyer that involved the consumption of copious amounts of alcohol and a competition to see who could speak the loudest; in which they all spoke at once and nobody listened. These parties were normally an all-male affair, and both the parties and the students were the bane of Min's life. Min was the short, wild-eyed auntie who lived in a tiny room behind the foyer's counter and was responsible for the upkeep, security, and safety of the whole building and its residents. Her long, wispy black hair was streaked with grey, and she was often seen wearing an apron and yellow rubber gloves, always ready to rifle through the daily rubbish discarded from the building. A red plastic tray that I poured toffee onto and could not get off was painstakingly scrubbed by Min after she found it in the bins. I later saw it in her room, holding her plant pots. After this, if I had anything I had no use for, I would put it carefully next to the bins so that Min could claim it without having to root through fish bones, broken beer bottles, and soiled toilet paper. Unfortunately, in China, the plumbing isn't great so used toilet paper is put in bins and not down the loo. This makes Chinese toilets particularly unpleasant, as well as unhygienic.

I both pitied Min and was highly wary of her. She had few personal possessions, was mistreated by the students who routinely spilt beer all over the floors or broke a door in the downstairs toilet, seemed to get very little sleep, and hardly ever took a holiday. But she was also a very strong woman who immediately disliked anyone who couldn't speak Chinese (I couldn't), ignored you if it wasn't worth her trouble to help you (I wasn't worth her trouble), was downright rude when in a bad mood (which was most days), and held a spare key for every room in the building (a formidable thought). Twice, having come back from a holiday, I discovered my bed had been slept in and my shower used. A large bag of chocolate eggs I had carefully opened and counted, to give to my students at Easter, was suddenly several eggs short. I already knew Min had a sweet tooth. When a parcel arrived from England, she went the extra mile to deliver it to me personally, insisting on coming to my room and watching me open it. Evidently, she could read the English word *chocolate* on the label. Having opened my box of *Milk Tray* in front of her, it was rude not to offer her one. She went away with two handfuls. She was both artful and a child.

Two Japanese teachers lived in my building. They were like chalk and cheese; one was charismatic and slightly eccentric, who once startled his Chinese students by dressing up as a woman; the other was bashful and more retiring. I sat next to the latter on the school bus and got to know him a little. He was somewhat of a mystery to me. He was beyond retiring age in Asia and yet wanted to stay on in China and teach, although his salary was low and his living arrangements dire. His corridor housed the noisiest of the Congolese students, and his bathroom had a perpetual leak from the room above, so he had to open up an umbrella every time he brushed his teeth or shaved. He had a strict daily budget of what he could afford to spend and therefore ate every meal in the school canteen, where a bowl of rice cost two pence, and avoided buying fruit in what he regarded as the 'overpriced' corner shop, where a bunch of bananas cost twenty pence. If he wasn't teaching or meeting students, he stayed cooped up in his room, quite literally.

His reception from the Chinese was mixed. When I arrived in China, anti-Japanese sentiment was being stirred up. On my second weekend, I ventured out of my campus with two Chinese girls. We had decided to go into the city centre — I hadn't been there yet – but on walking to the bus stop, were forced to drop that plan and take refuge in the nearby history museum. The streets were blocked by hundreds of Chinese men angrily marching across the city. Some wore black balaclavas; others held placards and banners. Protests in China are illegal, but this one was endorsed from above. Japanese cars were smashed and turned over, restaurants vandalised, and there were stories of innocent bystanders whose phones were snatched out of their hands and smashed because they were a Japanese brand. At my university, there was a lockdown and the Japanese teachers were kept inside, watched over by the fiery Min, who rose to the occasion like a stumpy, irate phoenix from its nest of ashes.

My Japanese colleague told me stories of being spat at, of being refused service in a restaurant when he opened his mouth and it was evident from his speech that he was not Chinese, of being ignored or given cold treatment. I asked my freshman students to draw a picture to represent themselves. This was during the Diaoyu Islands dispute,[6] but I was still surprised that, among pictures of dreamlike homes in idyllic countryside and sorely missed family members, there were a few pictures of students

---

6   The Diaoyu Islands (Senkaku Islands) are uninhabited islands located in the East China Sea between Japan, China and Taiwan. All three countries claim the islands.

standing next to the islands with the caption '*Diaoyu Islands belong to China!*' and a large Chinese flag drawn in the background.

I took the school bus daily to the Northern campus, where my students lived and studied. It was a forty-minute drive on a good day, but it could take up to two hours coming back into the city during rush hour in the evenings. The campus was in an area that was due to be developed, surrounded by fields and the bare beginnings of building projects. The students were marooned. It was a long and uncomfortable journey on public transport into the city centre, so they very seldom bothered to do it. With nothing to do in the evenings and at the weekend, most students became lazy and slept, or watched movies, played computer games, and became somewhat disillusioned. Their student lives seemed so different from my own student life, where I was out every night doing something and there was no end of exciting activities to get involved in.

My favourite students to teach were the freshmen. Their classes began several weeks into the first semester, as they spent the first month or so kitted out in military uniform, marching around the campus in the blistering September sun. I watched them from the balcony of my teaching building, sweat pouring down their foreheads, skin already burnt black, and heads thrust back, singing some rousing national song. The weaker students often fainted. All undergraduate students in China have to take formal military training at the beginning of their university life. Although this was quite a harsh start to university life for my students, it did create a strong bond between them and a feeling of comradery as these small, bewildered individuals gelled together in order to survive such an ordeal. By the time they arrived in my classroom, they were slightly shell-shocked and homesick, but extremely relieved to be sitting in a class in an air-conditioned room. They were new; everything was unfamiliar, and therefore they were curious, albeit shy; many had never had a foreign teacher before. I'd start off trying to be strict, but that quickly melted away as we got to know each other. Perhaps I was never a brilliant language teacher, but there was plenty of laughter in my classes, and I came to really care for my students.

The best time of the year was exam time, at the end of the winter semester and before the summer holidays. Chinese students excel at cheating. Some Chinese teachers also excel at covert cooperation by enabling students to cheat. To avoid this, I wrote four different exam papers for my British Culture class. A student later said they were all very impressed when they discovered this! During the exams, I confiscated all phones. There was strictly no talking and no passing of rubbers. For the Oral English exams, I got to spend an uninterrupted ten minutes with each student, a rare novelty, and I used my exam questions to find out more about them.

I thought I'd stay in the English Department and at least see my very first freshmen through to their graduation four years later. But after eighteen months, things took quite a different turn. After finishing for the winter holidays, and whilst the students sat their last exams, a student sent me a message. *"How come you aren't teaching us next semester?"* she asked. This was news to me! After enquiries, I discovered both myself and an American teacher were being moved out of the English Department to make way for a new foreign teacher. The problem was that nobody knew quite what to do with us. After several trips to the Foreign Affairs Office, where the Foreign Affairs Officer (FAO) scratched his head and periodically expelled air from his nostrils, and a rather awkward goodbye hug from the Head of the English Department when I gave in the exam results, a job was suddenly created for me. I was given a class of five young teachers who shared an office together and were working on a research project. And I was also given the job of teaching their boss – a professor who was also one of the Chancellors – and his wife, in the evenings. So, from the humble and rather obscure English Department, tucked away on the Northern campus, I suddenly rose, overnight (or rather over the winter holiday), to teaching in the highest ranks of the University.

I created a whole new syllabus for my group of teachers, grandly titled *Cross-Cultural Communication*, in which we all got very confused with each other's cultures. The classes were highly informal, and although

I prepared notes, they mainly consisted of chatting. After class, which was about twice a week, we went for lunch in different restaurants across the city. Once we drove right out to the suburbs to a *Nong Jia Le* 农家乐 'Happy Farmer Home'[7] where we ate plates of home grown produce, freshly slaughtered ducks, and bread straight out of the oven. My teachers knew how to eat! Our classes were often cancelled because these teachers were so busy. I had to get used to this and learn how to be flexible. Outside of class, I sometimes played badminton with the two youngest teachers, who did not yet have children. On one occasion, we went to the Toilet Restaurant. This novelty restaurant was located on the top floor of a luxury shopping mall. The seats were all toilets; the décor was toilet brushes and taps; and the ice-cream arrived in plastic urinals. Whether psychologically induced or owing to the poor quality of the food, we all had funny stomachs when we came back.

I taught the Professor and his wife for two and a half years, using one textbook, which we only got halfway through. They were also extremely busy people, so class was sometimes cancelled, or we went out for a meal instead because they hadn't eaten any dinner. Perhaps we got to know each other really well because of this spontaneity and informality. As I was studying Chinese, we spoke in a mixture of Chinese and English, the two blending seamlessly together. They lacked confidence speaking English when we started our classes, but by the end of our time together, I was listening to the Professor read speeches he had made in English to welcome visiting scholars. There's nothing quite like the sense of achievement that comes from seeing a student make progress!

The Professor was a short, slim man with eyes that crinkled when he smiled and he had a persistent, dry cough. Although I never used it, I gave him the English name Moses because it sounded similar to his Chinese name. When I explained about the name and how it had belonged to a man of humble birth who had become a leader of his people, he appeared quite chuffed. His wife already had an English

---

7   A form of rural tourism where farmers open up a restaurant and/or hotel on their land or in their home for city dwellers.

name. She was tall, with pale skin and shiny hair, elegantly coiffured in a short, wavy bob. Although they were successful people, they were from ordinary backgrounds, without pretensions, and fond of a good laugh. We had several good Christmas and Easter lessons in which they both asked many questions. Once, the Professor stated that he would like to believe in Jesus Christ in the future. Then, on our very last Christmas lesson, his wife said she thought it was true that Jesus was the Son of God. I left that lesson feeling a bit stunned, not knowing how to proceed. I prayed about suggesting we study the Bible in our lessons, but then the Professor was called away to Beijing for three months of mandatory Party meetings[8] so we didn't have any lessons for a long time. When we resumed, the feeling was gone, and then, a few months later, I went home.

---

8 It seems that the Communist Party periodically have meetings for educators, perhaps to relay new thinking and ideology to them.

Chapter 6

The Countryside

农村

I loved the countryside the best. It was full of old people, tottering about on sticks, as wizened as the land, or sitting on wooden stools in the shade of a house. The children were grubby and lively, and the rows of single storey houses ended abruptly in piles of bricks and worn-out slippers. At the edge of the village lay the graveyard, almost overcome by heaps of rubbish, its dusty old mounds crumbling into sand, marked only by strips of coloured plastic fluttering in the wind.

Sue's Village

I went to Sue's village with Grace at Lantern Festival. We were like visiting dignitaries. When we arrived, her family whisked us away to a tiny restaurant, where we ate lunch in the semi-darkness. On the way to the village, we sat in the back of an old, red trailer, balanced precariously on plastic stools, our faces whipped by the cold breeze. The whole village turned out to perform a dance for us. Old men in blue cloth caps beat massive red drums in time to the women, dressed all in pink, who danced round and round, waving their fans and bouncing their pink parasols up and down. We joined in towards the end. Then Sue asked us to perform something. Put on the spot, our brains raced; neither of us could yodel, dance the tango, or do the splits. We ended up singing *Jingle Bells* – the first verse through twice – because we'd both forgotten the next part. The onlooking villagers smiled politely but didn't comment. In the evening, we lit lanterns and watched them float up and away, becoming tiny dots of red light among a multitude of glittering stars.

The next day, there was a fair in town. I won three or four stuffed toys in a hoopla game. The vendor, having lost too many prizes in one go, crossly told us to move on. People were curious about us. A determined female teacher with a severe bob invited us to the local middle school. Accompanied by Sue, we ended up in a formal meeting with the headmaster and several teachers, eating peanuts and sipping green tea while giving advice about learning English. We were shown around the school and took turns being photographed playing ping pong with some of the pupils. The school supplied us with our own private photographer for the rest of our stay, lunch at a fancy restaurant, and a car and driver to take us to a mountain the following day. On the mountain, we met a guide, Zhao Yi, who insisted on accompanying us on all our subsequent excursions. For the next four years, he would magically reappear every time I visited Sue's village and almost every time I threw a party, even though he lived three hours from my city and was never personally invited.

Sue's grandfather had a museum just outside her village – an old stone house that sat amongst fields of wheat and cabbages, with huge stone dragons guarding its beautifully carved gate. He was a small man in a Mao suit who spoke fluent French and smoked like a chimney. His museum was crammed full of relics he'd salvaged from the Cultural Revolution, when the Red Guards were ordered to destroy anything that had traditional value. There were ornate mahogany chairs and wedding sedans covered in gaudy red silk, a large four-poster oak bed, and a garden filled with old stones chiselled into monkeys and lions and engraved with spirals of ancient calligraphy. Sue's grandfather spoke very highly of Mao, having been a Red Guard himself, despite the fact that his cherished relics in the museum would have been long lost if Mao's orders had been totally obeyed, and he himself would have been disciplined if he had got caught salvaging them. He was just one of the many contradictions that I met in China.

In Sue's village, we washed our hair in tubs of hot water, brushed our teeth out in the yard, and went to the toilet in a deep hole in a shack at the bottom of the garden, which had a door that didn't shut properly and a mound of used toilet paper rotting to one side. Although it was winter, we ate outside at a little wooden table, wiping the crumbs onto the floor when we were finished, which were promptly hoovered up by a dog or pecked at by chickens. I met Sue's aunts and uncles, her neighbours, and anyone else who happened to be passing by and wanted to enquire about the foreigners. Every gift I gave to Sue was divided among her relatives. A necklace went to one auntie, its matching earrings to another, and clothing to her mother. All the stuffed toys I'd won at the fair were carried off triumphantly by her small cousins.

In the summer, Zhao Yi took us to a village swimming pool. It resembled more of a pond. The water was dark green, and reeds grew along the edges. Sue and I sat on the edge, wetting our toes in the dank water. Sue was too embarrassed to wear a swimming costume, and I was put off by the state of the water to venture any further in. A few men lazily floated by on their backs or on large black rubber rings, with cigarettes dangling out of their mouths and beer bellies popping out of the water like the heads of hippopotamuses. Small boys ran about naked. Zhao Yi and his eighteen-year-old cousin grinned, hooted, and splashed about in the water like they were children again.

Kent's Village

About six months later, Sue met Kent, her first boyfriend. He was tall and dark, with jet-black hair that stood upright like a thousand spikes on the top of his head. Within a few months, he invited us both to his hometown, a village in a province that is (supposedly) full of thieves, peasants, and Christians. Sue explained that this visit to meet his parents was, traditionally, the beginning of their engagement. During the visit, money was exchanged as well as bottles of alcohol. I was given one too, which later blew the socks off my Grandad and still stands, collecting dust, on a shelf in his kitchen.

We took the overnight train to the nearest city, sleeping scrunched up on seats because it was cheaper than buying tickets for beds. We arrived stiff and grumpy at a train station that looked like a set in a cowboy film, and on exiting the station, we were accosted by many small, swarthy men trying to give us a ride in their taxis. We ate the local speciality for breakfast; beef noodles and fried bread. Wandering the outskirts of the city, we discovered a place with beautiful grounds dotted with ancient architecture, including a theatre that had once belonged to a poet or a Mandarin. There were rows of trees covered with red ribbons, white bridges over dark green ponds, and bright, bold murals of deer and herons. I woke up in those grounds; the heaviness of a night without sleep on a rocking train slipped away, and I was pleasantly surprised by such a gem in an otherwise dull and unremarkable city.

Kent's hometown was a village surrounded by reeds and ditches. We went for a walk and spotted a few ducks in the undergrowth. Kent drove us around on his motorbike; all three of us squeezed on, and once we even took his small nephew. When I was passed this little boy with a chubby face and red cheeks, I promptly passed him on. He always wore split bottom pants, so there was no knowing when he might go. Sue often got wet jiggling him on her knees. Nappies are still fairly uncommon in China. Babies are often swaddled in cloths and toddlers wear trousers with splits in so they can toilet on the side of the pavement or wherever they happen to be.

Sometime after this trip of fast motorbike rides along a large river and brilliant yellow balloons in the shady alcoves of a temple, Sue and Kent broke up. Apparently, he beat her. And then he got involved in a gang selling contraband. I'm not sure if Sue's family had to pay back any money or return any bottles of wine.

Katy's Village

During my second winter in China, Katy invited me to her village, way up in the northernmost reaches of a northern province in mainland China, almost a day's journey by coach from the largest city across yellow plains and sandy brown plateaus. This was where Mao set up his headquarters after the long march across China, and where people still live in caves. We passed the Great Wall on the coach – tumble down mounds of small, dark bricks, a far cry from the huge ramparts and wide staircases at the other end near Beijing. On the coach, Katy recounted to me the atrocities that the Japanese had done to the Chinese. She remembered every sordid detail and violent act that she had ever read about in the school textbooks or watched on TV – rape, mass murder, torture. She told me these stories while patting her ginger hair and munching on *ma hua* 麻花 'twisted, fried pretzels.'

I went to Katy's village to teach. She rented a small room that had a blackboard and a rusty pipe stove, which we fed with used yoghurt pots and old pieces of homework. A few doors down, there was a hairdresser where we paid fifty pence to get our hair washed because Katy's home, although brand new, did not have a working shower. Katy's family used to live in a mountainous area in one room that also, at certain times of the year, housed their goats. Katy later showed me this area when we went to a wedding there. Her new house was bought with dirty money from oil drilling by her dad, who no longer needed to work and instead spent his time drinking and seeing his mistresses. Katy's house was surrounded by other recently built homes (all empty shells), which was a suburb for the newly rich, sitting on the edge of a bleak, windswept village. It felt like a ghost town. For a newly built house, it was odd that nothing worked, not even the toilet. Although there were many rooms, her dad, mother, grandfather, and little cousin, all lived in one room, in which there was a stove, a small TV, and a large brick bed, like a platform, heated underneath by a coal fire. All four slept on this bed, also known as a *Kang* 炕. I never saw the grandfather rise from it. He was always smothered in heavy black clothes and a thick, oily jacket, with long black socks and a cloth cap perched on his bald head. Katy and I slept in her room, which was empty apart from a bed, thick duvet, and heat lamp. In the mornings, we had to fight with the duvet to roll it up in a certain way, and I had to put all my things away in my suitcase and hide it so that the room was completely decluttered, just in case any of the poorer villagers came round to marvel at the insides of this costly house.

Not having a toilet in the house was a great inconvenience. We had to make do with a plastic bowl. Katy emptied it every morning. In the daytime, we could use the village toilets – wooden shacks erected over six holes, all in a line without any partitions, the dirt floor covered in human waste and shockingly slippery. Dogs wandered around outside.

The children who came to the school were all dark-faced and exposed to the harsh elements. The sky was always a brilliant blue, and the sun always hung big and brazen over the crumbly yellow roads and grimy yellow buildings. In the mornings, we taught them simple English phrases, and every afternoon, selected one or two to take us to their homes where they could practise these phrases: *"This is my sister." "This is my grandfather; he is sixty years old."* In this way, within a week, I had visited ten or more local homes. Most of the children lived with their grandparents, other relatives, or family friends; their own parents having migrated to the cities to make a better living. They were *liu shou er tong* 留守儿童 'left-behind children', staying behind to take care of things. This drought-stricken dust plain was apparently a gold mine for oil. There were oil drilling rigs dotted about the countryside, but only a very few benefitted from the wealth they generated. My students wore the same clothes the whole week, washed their sooty faces in bowls of water, and slept in the same beds as their brothers and sisters. On my last day, we organised a party. In the village shop, we bought crisps, sunflower seeds, apples, and little yellow cakes full of air. The children came to Katy's house and shyly picked at the snacks. In the yard, I taught them *Duck, Duck, Goose,* and then we went to a nearby building site, deserted and silent, and played a wide game that left us breathless and hot in the chill air.

The Professor's Village

The Professor told me often about his *lao jia* 老家 his 'place of origin'. The concept of roots and origins holds strong in China. Many people live in cities far from the rural places where they grew up or where their parents and grandparents lived and died. The Professor's beginnings were humble. A small shack in the marshy expanses of damp *Sichuan* 四川, a province known for its hot, fiery food, peppered with chillies; its dark, green vegetation; and its warm, wet air. The Professor said its men are small and slight, and its women are beautiful. Perhaps their skin absorbs all the moisture; they glow with health. Growing up, the Professor had a sister, a pig, and a doting mother. Though they were dirt poor, he excelled at the tiny village school and passed the entrance exam for middle school in the nearest town. Unable to afford a bus ride, he'd walk an hour or two to get there. He only had one coat, and he ate just an egg for breakfast. Later, he made it to university. He refused to squander his money on going out to eat at restaurants like his classmates. He worked hard and eventually became a professor at a university. He moved his parents to the city, sent money to his sister's family, and bought a larger house in his hometown, keeping it in the village to remind him of where he came from.

It was the Spring Festival (Chinese New Year), and we stayed in a five-star hotel in a small city. I had a hot bath every evening, and there was a Western buffet in the morning, complete with toast, jam and coffee. From our place of comfort, we drove out to the village, where relatives congregated to *bai nian* 拜年 'pay a New Year call'. The village had no centre. Instead, it was a landscape of ponds and swamps, dotted with houses and criss-crossed with narrow, grassy paths. We spent a whole morning climbing up drenched hills to auspicious high spots where relatives were buried. Incense was lit, and fire crackers exploded, spraying drops of water through the air. The family bowed. After these rituals, we went to somebody's house. Wooden tables had been erected in the yard. Throughout the day, villagers arrived, and dishes flowed from the kitchen to feed them. Perhaps they shared the same surname.

Traditionally, villages in China were made up of individuals of the same surname, having descended from a common ancestor. These days, people perhaps presume on these distant, somewhat ancient 'connections' when they hear a good party is happening. We sat inside at a large round table, the doors wide open, feeding on fatty meat and wild vegetables.

In the evenings, back in the small city, we sat down to extravagant banquets with old colleagues, mayors, and the heads of the local army. We nibbled on oysters and caviar, sat on plush purple chairs, and toasted glasses of red wine. After the meal, we'd say goodbye and be dropped off at the hotel by the mayor or a jocular government official. We'd wait until he left, and then get a taxi to the city centre and eat steaming bowls of noodles outside at midnight, at small tables strewn across the pavement.

Angie's Village

My favourite village was Angie's. Angie was an enthusiastic student in my freshman class and a huge fan of Crazy English[9]. She got up at five every morning to read English aloud in the courtyard below her dormitory. She even started her own English corner and invited me to it. Angie was an ethnic minority, a Dong person (also known as the Kam-Sui people), and lived in the countryside of *Guizhou* 贵州 province. Angie lived in Zhaoxing, the largest Dong village with about eight hundred homes. I travelled south with Grace and somehow managed to find Angie's village after a long, bumpy bus ride out of Guiyang with only a packet of Oreos (we had no idea how far we were travelling) and terrible Chinese movies playing on the TV in which Chinese characters flew through the sky defeating evil spirits. We were dropped off on a large, dirty highway, a long way from anywhere, and surrounded by posters advocating the

---

9   A brand name for a non-traditional method of learning English, developed by Li Yang. Students are encouraged to go behind buildings or on rooftops and shout English. *"By shouting out loud, you learn"* is Li Yang's slogan. This way of learning is supposed to help students overcome shyness. It relies mainly on repetition so in that regard it's actually quite traditional.

Chinese Dream[10]. After a baffling ten minutes and a phone call, we got a lift to the border of Angie's village.

The village sat at the bottom of a series of hills that rose up out of the valley, one stacked upon another in an endless pile, until the very last pierced the sky. A river snaked its way through the village, crossed many times by wooden bridges, including 'wind and rain bridges,' wooden covered corridor bridges with pavilions and benches. In fact, the whole village was made of wood. The houses were built on stilts, three storeys high, with balconies and flat roofs where washing was hung out to dry. Outside in the yard, fires were lit in the evenings, and the older generation sat around them, grinning their toothless grins, and gossiping late into the night. Some of the cooking took place outside too, on huge woks over large stoves. Scattered throughout the village were wooden drum towers and pavilions. Fires were kept burning in their centres, and old men sat around them playing chess, smoking pipes, and chewing tobacco. Walking through the villages, I spotted women washing their hair in the icy river and others washing vegetables.

Across the vast hills were other Dong villages, accessible by steep mountain paths through a myriad of rice paddies. It was winter, so the rice paddies were still and silent, their murky grey depths reflecting the grey sky above them. On the road out of the village, we passed an old man carrying wicker baskets on his shoulders.

On the outskirts of the village, we came across a little hut. Inside, on a stone ledge, sat two handmade dolls in traditional costume, with pink skirts and dangly earrings. They were surrounded by offerings of fruit, dried flowers, fir cones, and feathers. Perhaps these figures represented Sa Sui, the land goddess. There were other shrines on our route, some more crude and rudimentary, with stone idols that resembled Easter Island heads, their little tables cluttered with old Coca Cola bottles, unused cigarettes, and the burnt remains of paper money.

---

10   中国梦 – a phrase popularised by Xi Jinping. According to the Party the Chinese Dream is about Chinese prosperity, collective effort, socialism and national glory.

Late one afternoon, we went to a performance of Dong dancing and singing. The women wore patterned sarongs over their embroidered skirts, silver ornamental headdresses, and silver breastplates. White ribbons were tied around their thick leggings. The men wore bronze turbans, short embroidered jackets, and sarongs over their brown trousers, from which dangled tawny feathers. Their voices rose over each other, blending together with the lutes and the stringed instruments. Angie said every Dong could sing. They spend most of their lives singing and have songs about everything, all learnt by heart and sung from memory. When the men began to dance, I was somehow dragged into it. It was some sort of circular conga. Later, in true Dong tradition, my dad made up a song about this unique Dong experience:

'I danced with the Dong men,
I danced with the Dong men all that night.
I danced with the Dong men,
Those Dong men are alright.'

I don't think the Dong people would be impressed by his songwriting talent.

Chapter 7

This really is China!

这就是中国！

We foreigners had a certain expression we would use when anything incredible or just downright 'bonkers' happened in China (which was most of the time). In our poor Chinese, with the accent wrong and the tones all muddled, we would exclaim with arms raised or eyes wide with disbelief, "这就是中国！ *This really is China!*" This was a phrase that encapsulated our feelings of being fish out of water and aliens in a strange land, as well as the ever-common realisation that we were almost always slightly out of touch with what was really going on. Life in China was full of moments that seemed like excerpts from episodes of Mr Bean – somewhat comical and ludicrous, with an element of cringe! It helped, therefore, to have a good sense of humour.

The Dreaded Medical

When you move to China for the first time, and subsequently whenever you change your visa type, you must go for a medical. This takes place in a large, imposing government-style building that consists of many floors which are divided into booths and separate rooms. There is the ECG room, the eye test room, the room for testing blood pressure, and the blood test hatch, which is like a counter at a bank, but through which you stick your arm and part with some of your blood. The whole building smells of thick yellow substances and gauze. It is always chocka-block with bewildered foreigners, blinking in the white light and being prodded along from one booth to the next like pieces of meat in a factory. The nurses are as mechanical as workers on a production line and as communicative as pieces of machinery. With the vast array of ethnicities passing through the building hourly – Koreans, Pakistanis, Europeans, and Arabs – communication is reduced to pointing, pushing, prodding, and poking. What was unexpected, though, was the lack of privacy. This didn't matter much, apart from in the ECG room, where it mattered an awful lot. Two beds were separated from each other and from the rest of the room by flimsy white screens. Whoever was summoned to the second bed had to walk past the poor person in the first bed, baring it all. There was always much confusion. A huddle of Pakistani men would peer over the screen to bed one to see what was going on, perhaps unsure of what room they had entered and what exactly they were queuing up for. Or an impatient Taiwanese would barge into the booth to fire some rapid and angry Chinese at the nurse, not giving any consideration to the person staring grimly at the yellowed ceiling with wires stuck to their chest. Thankfully, after an embarrassing experience in my first medical, Sue came with me to my second and helped to keep any onlookers out. Sue was very handy to have around, especially when the nurse informed us that, according to the machine's reading, I didn't have any blood in my brain. She attempted another reading, with equally disastrous results, and then waved us away. I was a little concerned that my brain was without blood, but Sue said, *"That explains a lot,"* and therefore reassured me. Three days later, I received my all-clear medical card and was allowed to stay in China for another year, even though according to their medical, I was already dead.

The Cucumber Diet

In my first year in China, my students often told me I was too slim. They encouraged my love of milk tea, believing the sweet, milky drink would help me gain weight. They needn't have worried. After developing a love of Chinese food, it was hard not to put on weight. As most socialising revolved around food, and portion sizes were always large, it was very easy to fill out, expand, and increase a dress size. In my second year, both Sue and I were starting to feel the effects of too much food. Sue wasn't fat but was round with a comfortable plumpness. A trait that many countryside girls share. Sue bought a bike to help matters. We discussed exercising as we walked to the market to buy vegetables and to our favourite restaurant to get cold noodles with peanut sauce and vinegar. Then, towards the end of the summer, Sue, who hadn't been successful in losing weight despite the bicycle, decided on a more drastic plan. It was called *The Cucumber Diet*. She was staying at my flat at the time and suggested we stay together, locked inside, for a whole week. We wouldn't be allowed out during that time because outside was Temptation (in the form of many different foods and restaurants). Inside my room, we would have a large store of hairy, prickly cucumbers (a Chinese variety of the more commonly known salad cucumber) and water. For accountability, stickability, and moral support, we would have each other. Sue said we could just lie around, eating the prickly cucumbers, and our excess weight would just slip off. When we were overcome by hunger pangs or the sheer misery of another prickly cucumber, we could vent our frustration out on each other. Somehow, we would come through it and be able to leave the flat at the end of the week slim and attractive. As Sue explained all this, I had terrible visions of being stuck inside for a week with Sue and a large supply of cucumbers, of the two of us lying famished on the lilac sofa, or of Sue beating me over the head with a half-eaten cucumber. It sounded like the Worst Diet Ever. So, I pointed out that we would soon put the weight back on after the end of *The Cucumber Diet*. Sue suggested a Cucumber Diet Day every couple of weeks. Thankfully, I was unable to find a whole week where I was free enough to be locked away for seven days, so we shelved *The Cucumber Diet* idea and instead enjoyed extra helpings of shredded cucumber on our cold noodles with a can of coke.

My Name is British Citizen

In my last year in China, I ran out of money in my Chinese bank account. Not surprising as I was then a language student and not earning. So, I asked a friend to send money to me from the UK. However, when I went to collect the money from my bank, they refused to give it to me because the name on my bank account was not the name on my passport. This was news to me! I had opened my bank account in the very first week of my arrival in China, when the roads seemed impassable and I had to wait for two Chinese girls to take pity on me and guide me across, each holding onto an elbow; when the stares of strangers on the street still made me uncomfortable; and when I had still assumed that most people could speak a little English.

In that first week, my university sent me to the bank to open a bank account. The bank was small, tucked under a bridge that connected the residential campus of the university, where the teachers lived, with the teaching campus, where the classrooms, sports facilities, and student dormitories were. It was almost empty when I arrived. The guard on the door waved me in, his uniform and grey cap seeming too heavy for such a sticky August morning. From a machine, I received a slip of paper with a number on it. When it was my turn to go up to the counter, a speaker announced my number, and the girl behind the glass stood up and saluted. No one behind the counter spoke English, or if they did, they weren't willing to use it. I pointed at my passport and waved my teacher's ID card; they got the gist and opened a bank account for me. So easy, I thought – I don't need to know Chinese!

Three years later, I was back in the bank under the bridge and unable to withdraw my funds from England. Confused, I asked what name my account was under. They printed out a piece of paper. Under where it said 'name', it read *'British Citizen.'* The girl who had set up my account three years before, had mistaken my nationality for my name. And so ensued three months of visits to my bank, where I was told to bring different pieces of information each time, and several visits to other branches in the city. Eventually the problem was sorted out one afternoon after a four-hour wait while the staff scratched their heads, discussed the problem, and went on their lunchbreak. They finally managed to change my name to what it should have been all along, and I withdrew long-awaited money. Opening a bank account in China was never easy.

Midnight on the Wall

While living in China I had a fair few friends come to visit me and many opportunities to travel. Travelling in China however is not straightforward and not always tourist friendly - these excursions of ours often involved many scrapes. In one place we visited the ancient city wall. This wall is twelve metres high, fourteen metres wide, and covers eight miles in length. It has four main gates with towers and fortifications, aptly named the North Gate, the East Gate, the South Gate, and the West Gate. On summer evenings in this city, when the night air is warm and fuzzy, and the wall is lit up with huge red lanterns that glow softly in the dark, Chinese people like to walk leisurely along a section of the wall. To walk the whole wall would take about four hours.

I visited this wall with a German friend who came to China to see both me and the country, and my Chinese housemate who often was as equally bemused as me by any odd encounter or unforeseen obstacle that arose in our path. We arrived at the South Gate a little later than anticipated and were some of the last people to ascend it that evening. We ambled along, feeling the rough stones beneath our flimsy shoes, enjoying the music of lutes and zithers played from speakers along the wall, and peering over now and again to see the people below, dancing, singing, or exercising; their faces lit by yellow lights hid amongst the bushes. They were like shadow puppets that jumped and skipped and then were still again, disappearing into blackness until another took their place. After a while, we passed the East Gate and the last few people walking on the wall, going in the opposite direction. Out there, it was quieter;

there were no people down below singing or dancing, in fact, the further we walked, the more we were surrounded by silence and emptiness. Below the wall, there were no more parks, moats, ornamental stones, or silver trees. We appeared to be encompassed by construction sites and the shells of buildings. We each had a bottle of milk tea, and thus feeling quite content, although a little tired, we decided to keep walking and descend the wall at the North Gate. If the sky had been clear, there might have been some stars. Occasionally, we heard the sound of a car below on a road.

After some time, I realised we were walking in silence. The music from the speakers had been turned off. As soon as we noticed that, the lanterns along the wall went out one by one, leaving us in shadow, surrounded only by the distant blue and white lights of the city. Feeling slightly alarmed, we picked up our pace. Eventually, up ahead, we spotted the North Gate and made our way towards it, relieved, our feet now starting to feel the effects of so many cobbled stones. It turned out, however, that the North Gate was shrouded in darkness, and although there was a staircase leading down, it was fenced off and the gate padlocked shut. We were all rather hot and tired. The milk tea was almost gone. My German friend suggested climbing over the gate, but I couldn't find the courage for that course of action, imagining secret cameras monitoring our escape. Searching the vicinity, we discovered a small plaque with a phone number on it. Calling the helpline, my Chinese housemate spoke to a member of staff responsible for the wall. The staff member confirmed that the wall was now closed to tourists. We must descend immediately. We told him we were at the North Gate. He said we couldn't descend from the North Gate. We said we had just come to that realisation ourselves. What did he suggest we should do? He said all the gates were closed now, but one usually descends from the South Gate. Dismayed, we looked at each other. Another two hours walk back to the South Gate? I suggested that we call again and ask them to send a little buggy to pick us up. The wall had electric buggies that the staff drove. We made another call. A woman answered this time. She said the staff had all left for the night, and there was therefore no one available to drive a buggy for us. We asked the woman if she was willing, but no, she was leaving too. We'd best make our way to the South Gate. "*The South Gate is two hours away,*" we said. There might be someone at the East Gate who could let us out, she answered. So, we turned and made our slow way back to the East Gate.

It was about midnight when we arrived. This gate was also in total darkness. At the tower, we could descend stairs to the ground level, a large courtyard, but were barred from the road outside by a large metal gate, like the gate to a castle. We wandered around the courtyard in the pitch dark, calling out. When we called the helpline again, nobody answered. After a thorough search of the courtyard, we sank down onto the floor next to the gate, resolved to spend the night on, or rather in, the confines of the wall.

What would happen in the morning when we were discovered, we will never know, because after about half an hour of uncomfortable seating and discussions about how to ration our resources and keep warm in the wee hours, a security guard thrust his head through the gate and grunted at us, flashing his torch around as he fumbled in his pockets for keys to let us out. He'd been napping outside in a little cabin and had just happened to look up at the CCTV screen when stretching in his chair to see three young women huddling inside the East Gate, looking out disconsolately from between the bars.

Chapter 8

Straight Ahead Bravely

勇往直前

I first met the teenagers when Grace asked me to help her take them swimming. Of course, I'd heard a lot about them before that first encounter. One always heard about these teens – and indeed heard the teens themselves – before actually seeing them. These teenagers were a mixed bunch of orphans, with various special needs and learning difficulties. They were taken out of government institutions and placed in a home. I often thought of them as small soldiers, for not only were they carrying with them wounds from their past (neglect, abandonment, abuse), but they were also battling every day of their lives against a society that for the most part saw them as less than human and therefore a burden, or as an embarrassment that should be shut away somewhere; cared for in some ways, but hidden and forgotten by most. In their own school, they learnt life skills, simple maths, and Chinese, but Saturday morning swimming was by far their favourite activity. Whenever they bumped into me during the week, they'd always ask, *"Are you going swimming?"* even if it happened to be Monday. And they did bump into me – quite literally. On catching sight of me down the road, a mad stampede would ensue. They'd all run towards me, and I'd freeze. Then there was a domino effect as the fastest stopped just shy of me and the rest crashed into him, sending them all toppling. The teens were all scraped knees, flailing limbs, and loud voices – a whirlwind of constant action and excitement that left you slightly stunned with your hair flattened and your thoughts undone as they passed on.

We took the local bus to the swimming pool. The bus was a badly dented box on wobbly wheels. The bus stop just happened to be outside a small bakery that spilled out onto the pavement, so it was a constant struggle to keep the boys away from the baskets of buns. When the bus arrived, we all swarmed onto it – a handful of volunteers and about eight or more teenagers. After a twenty-minute bumpy ride, where teenagers collided into each other and volunteers lost their footing, we'd all tumble out at the pool.

In the pool, I was paired with Lisa - a short, stocky girl as stubborn as a bull and as strong as an ox. She held my shoulders and tried to kick. When Daniel caught sight of her, he made a beeline for us. Panicking, Lisa grappled with me and attempted to hide behind me, while I had a few seconds to wonder how I was going to fend Daniel off as his well-built form waded towards us at an alarming speed (as far as wading goes). Thankfully, a volunteer came to the rescue, diving at Daniel and *taking him out* as the two of them disappeared under the water for a few seconds.

The highlight of Saturday morning swimming was doing the hokey cokey and walking fast in a circle so as to create a mini whirlpool. With these energetic boys and strapping girls throwing their arms and legs up in the air and splashing with great gusto, it was a surprise that the pool itself wasn't half emptied and the lifeguard wasn't half-drowned on the side of the pool. The pool was closed to the public while we were there, and the only staff were the lifeguard, who casually sauntered around in his small pair of trunks, and the plump lady who sold the tickets, frilly swimming costumes with skirts attached and plenty of bows, and bottles of Lipton iced tea. After a few weeks of volunteering with the teenagers, during which I was once paired with Samuel and nearly drowned when he used me as a float, I was asked to help take the toddlers swimming instead. I accepted this as a much easier alternative that didn't involve a gallon of swallowed water or any actual swimming or diving. Swimming with babies had a magical ring to it. I still saw the teens when we took the babies out of the water. They waited on the side, their legs twitching impatiently, before entering the pool en masse, falling through the air like lead balloons.

Later, we moved into a flat that was two buildings in front of the boys' home. I could hear them in the morning when I got up. Samuel's voice echoed through the buildings; his words indistinct but the booming tones clearly his – he could have functioned as my personal alarm clock. The teenagers could be spotted throughout the day in the neighbourhood, either walking to school in the morning, dragging their feet, or coming home for a midday nap. After school, James might be spotted dangling from a tree or rifling through the hordes of rubbish that daily built up in Rubbish Lane – the pathway that ran alongside a small play area to the side gate and onto the road. Rubbish Lane daily received such gifts as old mattresses with their springs poking out, cracked bathtubs, and plenty of glass bottles. The pavement in Rubbish Lane was permanently dyed a dark, sluggish brown; your shoes stuck to it as you treaded your way carefully around the worse areas. In the evening, in the half-light, the boys were sometimes seen carefully carrying a huge saucepan of soup and a large bowl of noodles as they wound their way through Rubbish Lane to the girls' flat with their evening meal. If I happened to pass them when they were carrying food, I often ended up with a dry steamed bun pressed into my hand.

Once on my way home, I happened to come across the boys huddled around something on the ground. Elbowing my way in, I discovered James crouched down with a very badly mangled dog in his arms. The teenagers had rescued a dirty stray. During the course of a few days, the boys, though mainly James, tried to raise the dog in one of the basements on the housing estate. After a while, James tried to palm the flea-infested dog off on me. In the end, the boys seemed to lose interest in the dog, and the security guard took him away.

I got to know the teenagers better when I taught them how to bake. In our early lessons, we used a large table in the main room of their school, where Samuel grated his thumb into the cake along with the carrots. Eventually, we had a room especially for baking, kitted out with all the necessary equipment, including chef outfits for the students. Bill loved to use the electric whisk and probably would have been quite content to stand there all day, whisking up eggs, laughing, and trying to control the thing as it whizzed up and down and around the bowl. The teens became excellent bakers as they practised the same recipes for weeks and weeks, perfecting fairy cakes and creating Michelin-style biscuits.

An English lesson was added to my timetable when Lucas asked me to teach him English. This was before he went back to the AWC. The English lesson meant forgoing his midday nap, but he was so keen to learn English that he didn't mind. He really admired a Chinese man who lived with the boys as a helper. This man had learnt English partly through reading the Bible.

I loved to hang out with these young people and to visit them after school hours. When the teenagers found out where I lived, they sometimes turned up on my doorstep! When Lucas came to my flat one day, I was busy cooking. He took one look at the food in my wok and uttered a loud *"Oh no!"* He told me the food was unpalatable and that he was henceforth going to teach me how to cook. He then gave me specific instructions on what ingredients to buy and a time and date for our lesson at the house he shared with the other boys. Lucas turned out to be a great teacher, though a little bossy, but he was an even better cook, and he taught me how to make fried garlic shoots with pork. We ate it around their kitchen table, the fat oozing out of the pork and the crunchy garlic shoots bursting with the soy sauce they'd soaked up in the wok. Unfortunately, this was both our very first and last cookery lesson, as Lucas was reprimanded by his teachers for arranging a *'secret class.'* I was slightly alarmed when I first saw the height of the flames on his stove, but he handled them so well, despite difficulties with his mobility, that I was actually very impressed.

A friend donated a bicycle to the teenagers, so we decided to teach them how to ride. One afternoon, a Chinese volunteer and I led the way to the park, wheeling the bicycle along as, with much excitement, the teens ran on in front. We headed straight for the bicycle repairman who always took up station next to the public toilets. He was a lean, dark man with a hawk-like face; his clothes greasy and stained, and his hands always covered in a tar-like substance. He had a cigarette safely tucked behind his ear and one dangling from his lips. He got to work fixing a new bicycle seat and pumping up the tyres, bombarded by questions from James. He knocked off a large percentage of the price because the bicycle was for the teenagers. When it was ready, I looked around for everybody. The park was busy with elderly people sitting on the walls chatting, and children at various stalls painting papier-mâché fish and tigers. Groups of teenage boys were playing basketball on the courts. When we finally rounded up all the children, we realised that Daniel wasn't there. James said he might have gone to the toilet, so we sent him in to look. But no, he wasn't there. We went back to the housing estate to give a cycling lesson to two of the boys. Apart from ending up in the bins a few times, they took to cycling really well. We played around for a while, waiting for Daniel, but he still hadn't turned up. I was beginning to have a horrible feeling that I might have lost him. A search party was sent out. I went home, but after a few hours, I felt like I ought to be searching too. There was no news of Daniel, and some local sisters had gone out in a car to scout the area. It was now early evening. Then, as I was walking carefully down Rubbish Lane, I spotted a figure hiding behind one of the corners of a tower block of flats opposite the Lane. It was Daniel, lurking in the shadows. I waved at him, and he quickly disappeared behind the building, grinning and skulking at the same time. When I called a member of staff, he wasn't surprised that Daniel was both not very far away and having a whale of a time absconding. I'm not sure when they eventually caught up with him or what disciplinary measures were dished out, but I do know that this wasn't the last time Daniel played the escapee.

I got to know some of the teenagers well. Lucas, of course, because I spent more time with him. And Bill, because he often accompanied me on walks, chattering about how sweet potato fries are unhealthy and therefore I shouldn't buy them anymore. When Bill was in a particularly amiable mood, especially if it happened to be a festival, he sometimes gave me a kiss on the cheek. He was a typical spotty teenager who usually happened to have the remains of his lunch around his mouth and a permanently congested nose that was crusty around the edges. The teenagers were affectionate at times. When I was sitting next to Lisa on a wall, watching the others play, she surprised me by tenderly patting my arm and resting her head on my shoulder. It was a beautiful moment where I saw a different side to her, gentle and tender, but then she went and spoiled it by sticking one of her fingers up my nose.

These young people were a joy to be with and a messy delight to care for. When they laughed, you couldn't help but laugh along too. But of course, they carried deep wounds, hurt and anger that sometimes surfaced unexpectedly and manifested in behaviour that could be challenging, ironically more so as they found themselves in loving and safe environments. Their caregivers needed great wisdom and as much bravery as the teenagers themselves. It was wonderful to witness, slowly, day by day, some of these teenagers flourish, grow, mature and develop into healthier and happier individuals. One of the girls was adopted to the US. Dancing in the living room of her new home with all her new little brothers and sisters around her was such a joy to see. I used to dance with her too, twirling round and round in the middle of the floor. God had rescued another life. To see photos of the boys working outside, strong and tanned by the sun, active and engaged, growing in so many ways, expanding in different directions, warmed my heart. God provides homes for the deserted; however unconventional these homes may appear to be to the outsider. Yet if God's people are there, then so is His presence. All He requires of us is to move ahead bravely, obedient to His call, straight ahead despite misunderstanding and sometimes hostility. Even though these young people had been unwanted or, for whatever reason, were unable to be kept by their families, even though they were disabled and obscure, just one out of hundreds or even thousands of abandoned children in China, yet God sees each one and He does care. He is the helper of the fatherless and the Father of the orphan. The love of a good God evident in the lives of these teenagers and through the givenness of their caregivers would later encourage me many times - knowing that I too am held, not just in the hands of God, but in His thoughts and heart.

Chapter 9

A Sensitive Soul

一个敏感的灵魂

'It is both a blessing
And a curse
To feel everything
So very deeply.'

Many of the people I met in China were poets and philosophers at heart. They seemed to feel things very deeply and were able to compact intense emotion and experience into words and sentences. China is, after all, a nation of poets and has been for thousands of years. In ancient China, scholars whiled away precious hours sipping green tea and composing poetry under the magnolia trees, and in modern China, young people still write poetry.

Marta was already a third-year student when I taught her. She was small and serious, with round metal glasses and a tendency to pause and think and then frown slightly before answering you. She took me to the ancient Buddhist pagoda on a crisp, sunny morning when the autumn leaves had just begun to fall. She will forever be associated with autumn and with leaves in my memory because of the book of leaves she made and her often expressed desire to lie buried and still under the orange leaves that crunched beneath our feet. Marta collected shells and smooth stones, and she grew spider plants in plastic bottles on her desk. When I visited her, she always made me flower tea. She also gave me her spare duvet – a large, green-padded duvet that looked like a relic from the Chinese Civil War – the same duvet her father carried to her on a fourteen-hour train ride from her hometown. When we met, we always walked around the grounds of the various campuses she lived on. We read poetry together, and, when she moved nearer to me, we read the book of Ecclesiastes, a book that speaks so much to the Chinese heart. It spoke to Marta too, and it seemed to answer every question or confusion she voiced on our walks around the university, but her heart was still hard, and she could not acknowledge this. She fell deeper into depression, feeling isolated and unable to trust anyone. One warm afternoon, she broke down and clung to me in the soft silence of her empty dormitory. I'd never seen such grief before. From then on, I was able to pray with her.

Spring Flower, Autumn Moon

Less beautiful than you
The summer rain, the winter snow
Thankful to Heaven that we met and know each other
May our friendship grow with time
May you walk calmly through the four seasons
Without sorrow, without fear.

Jolene's hometown was full of carved yellow stones, and at night, the pale-yellow moon was reflected in the brown waters of the river. Jolene had a round face and cropped hair, like a boy, and she liked to laugh, but under all her mirth there was a steady current of melancholy. She took me to walk on the soft grey hills that looked down on the town as the sun went down, and we passed graves in lonely spots, while in the distance, horns and discordant pipes were played by shadows in the twilight. Jolene was often ill and disappeared at different times. Her mother was an alcoholic, addicted to gambling in mah-jong[11] dens, and her father was often drunk too. She believed her ancestors were cursed because they all died young; maybe, she said, because one of

---

11 A Chinese tile-based game and popular for gambling.

them was a Feng Shui master in touch with spirits. Jolene sometimes read the Bible with me. One evening she came to my flat, and I gave her a book called *Redeeming Love*.[12] This book transports the Biblical story of Hosea marrying Gomer, the prostitute, to California in the 1850s and follows the story of a young Christian man who falls in love with a prostitute called Angel. I bought this book in a Christian bookshop when the bookseller pressed it into my hands at the till, saying, *"This is the book you were looking for."* I was buying cards, not books, and thought she must have mistaken me for someone else, but I bought it anyway. When Jolene returned the book, she told me she couldn't put it down. She said she felt the love of God pouring from the walls and filling her room. Jolene struggled with sleeplessness and fear. When she slept in my flat, she lay awake in the small hours of the night listening to someone crying, which the rest of us couldn't hear. She sometimes heard voices and complained of a pain like a stone that rolled down her leg. When she wasn't nearby, she often sent me messages crying out for help and was often besieged by a paranoia that someone around her would harm her. *"This makes me want to kill myself,"* she said. Jolene longed for something in her life to give the dull greys and yellows, colour. Continually, she was pointed to Jesus. It seems most Chinese long for *'a colourful life'* (a Chinglish expression by which they mean a life full of meaning). But it's only Jesus who can give us such colour.

---

12 Redeeming Love by Francine Rivers

Chapter 10

A Glimpse

一瞥见

I am not a writer or a novelist, per se. I am a poet, and as a poet, China spoke to my soul. There was a beauty and a richness I found in China that I had lost in this familiar Northern world of wet green fields and gardens damp with dew at dawn. It was almost like the world came and found me and I experienced life again, like it was the first time, fresh and new and a little surprising. I felt fully present in China and fully alive. And what I saw, heard, and experienced, touched something deep inside me that had always been there, dormant. It woke up, uncurled, and came alive.

Not only did life somehow feel like it was rich and vibrant and full of meaning, but I also felt that, perhaps for the first time in my life, I was seen, validated, embraced, and loved for being myself by a people other than my own.

What follows in this chapter are glimpses of China in the language of my heart – more poetic than prosaic.

Home City:

City of rest, rest as long and as ancient as the mountains themselves; where the people bustle and the cars narrowly miss your bicycle. Huge roads like enlarged veins pull traffic in and out of the centre, the *zhong xin* 中心, 'heart of the city'. The buildings all look the same. If you can see mountains, you're looking south. It's boiling hot except when it's cold, and it's yellow; yellow streets and yellow stores. There's colour where the sheep are slaughtered on the side of the road. Little splatters of rich red, but the sheep carcass is already yellow in the drain. We are dwarfed by gigantic buildings and statues of Tang dynasty emperors. The fountains dance to classical music, and the guards blow their whistles when a boy runs out to touch the water. When it rains, it floods. When it snows, carpets appear on the bridge. In winter, even the trees have their own blankets. They speak like birds here, but they squat like children. They eat like kings, but they look like peasants. And the yellow is dry and crumbling.

My washing machine flooded the kitchen. The shower head exploded like a bomb, spraying fragments of white shrapnel through the air. The light shade was held up by pieces of yellowed sellotape, but it never once fell on my head. This is the city of the long dead, where children play on the grassy tombs of ancient rulers, but the elderly whisper *Zhe ge difang hen xie* 这个地方很邪 'this place is evil'. This is a city swarming with students and scholars and schools. In the dark of a mosque, men are wringing their hands. At the top of a mall, a girl is longing to jump. In hundreds of hired rooms across the city, graduate boys are drinking weak beer and singing sad songs. Outside the library, Rodin's The Thinker thinks his endless thoughts. In the park next to the railway station, aunties hang pictures of nieces and nephews from the trees, hoping to find a suitable spouse, and by the fading light of the sun, we bury Leslie's dead turtle in the communal back yard.

Hangzhou 杭州 :

City of heaven; with its balmy evenings and dishes of sweet fish. The windows are always flung open. Petals fall over the lake like grains of round rice, and at every turning the water and trees look like another perfect Chinese painting. They say here that a white snake became a white woman and spent her days looking longingly out of a tower window. Perhaps she could see her pale face beneath her in the waters. But it might have only been the moon. There are tulips everywhere, bright yellow and bold red. We take photos with every flower. This is the city of green tea and deep wells of clear water, where the tea grows stronger after every mouthful. In the Old District, the houses are whitewashed and the street slants up to meet the sky. A wooden boat drifts slowly on the canal, whilst fat raindrops fall from the engraved eaves of overhanging houses. In the fair, there are men dressed as warriors, a bedraggled monkey climbs up a ladder, and we sit on benches to drink yellow wine from small bowls of silver. This is the city of opera and acrobatics, of poets and players. In the morning, we steam custard buns and eat purple porridge.

Beijing 北京：

City of contradictions and people. There are people everywhere, holding brightly coloured parasols under a scorching sun, like a kaleidoscope of quivering butterflies, or holding high dark umbrellas and sodden newspapers as the angry sky lets fall its deluge. Lightning flashes across the sky, and the cheap hotel room quakes with a roll of thunder. There are portraits of Mao everywhere; large and miniscule, painted and printed, sculpted in stone, and mass produced in plastic. But in the 798 Art District, he stands decapitated. We queue to see his corpse covered in white roses. We wander from courtyard to courtyard in the Forbidden Palace, dazed and exhausted, and make countless coke-guzzling trips to McDonald's. This is the city of great constructions and small dwellings, of walls, gates, and doors, of alleyways, and basements for the poor. We eat duck dripping with fat and crunch thin scorpions between our teeth. I buy crushed pearls to drink that will make my skin radiant, but in the furnace-like heat, we are all melting. We consume countless rare dishes at a banquet and multiple packets of Oreo biscuits. We see the Empress Dowager Cixi's extravagance – her lakes and her temples and her stone-bottomed boat – and we're stared at and photographed by hordes of countryside folk.

Guilin 桂林：

City of skinny mountains and lazy rivers. Old men sit under osmanthus trees playing chess or fall asleep on huge rocks in the shade. We roll up our dresses, paddle under a waterfall, and climb alongside donkeys that are laden with bricks up steep stairs and rice terraces. A Yao woman unties her long hair while she sings. We eat frogs for lunch. Outside the restaurants, fat guinea pigs doze in wire cages. On a listless afternoon, the glass ceiling shatters. This is the city whose scenery is stamped on paper currency. We take a bamboo raft down the river and ride bicycles around mountains, rocks, and hills. In a cave, we bathe in thick mud and at night, buy boiled crab on a stick.

Chengdu 成都：

City of treasures; of Tibetan teapots and sleepy pandas, of wide lanes and narrow ways, quiet courtyards, and teeming monasteries where prayers float on the coils of smoke that rise from the oil burning in a hundred golden vessels. We watch the women kneel to pray and place flowers on the altar. The monks, robed in orange, stand before tables laden with apples and oranges and candles shaped like pink lotus flowers that weep hot wax as they gradually melt away. The air is intoxicated with incense. This is a city full of religion. We stand at the foot of the Giant Buddha, who towers above us; his fingers are longer than me. They say he is looking out across the rivers, but to me he looks drowsy, like he's falling asleep. In the dark recesses of a small café, we chew on yak and sip butter tea that's thick like syrup. A dark man with a flat face picks up a stringed instrument, plays a song and asks for money. In the park, old men nibble on melon seeds and sip green tea. They pay a pittance to have their ears cleaned by a man with a metal tong. The Min River is artic blue; mist rises from its surface. The trees are dressed with icy jewels; it's silent in the forest. Every night, the auntie bathes her feet in a bucket of boiling water. I watch her sigh as I brush my teeth. The steam from the Hot Pot we eat blows in my face so that my skin is wet and glistens. There is so much water in this city– in the air and on our skin, it thickens hair and makes the women beautiful.

Kunming 昆明：

City of spring. There are cherry blossoms in the park and the streets are full of soft sunshine. It's February, but we hang our washing on the roof to dry. This is a city dappled with light. At the top of the Western hills, the wind blows strong, but the sun still shines brightly over the waters below. Every crevice has a crumbling statue, and every alcove is a dusty shrine. In the evening, we queue to eat fried goat's cheese and potato cakes. We lose ourselves for a whole day, wandering amongst the stones of the Stone Forest, enchanted by their shapes, sucked into a world of grey. It is like walking through an old castle, full of shadows and gloom, hemmed in by heavy walls of limestone. And then we stumble across a group of Sani women in bright red and blue, and they are smiling and holding tubs of pink and yellow flowers, and we are back again in a world of colour and emotion.

In Dali 大理 we are like the men who dwelt at Dale, living beneath the Lonely Mountain. The mountain looms above us and the sky is full of wisps of smoke and cloud. Flags flap in the rough wind. We are on the edge of somewhere – a frontier. It took us ages to get here. There is a little Bai church with a white-walled courtyard. Inside, it is silent and still. At night, I sit outside on the balcony watching the stars. The air is so cold, but the beauty of the dark sky keeps me warm. We walk around wet villages and fields of thick grass the colour of fern, soft and damp. Everywhere smells of mist and smoke and the strong roots of mountains.

Chongqing 重庆：

City of abundance; of huge bridges and wide roads, and tall buildings that touch the clouds. At night, the city glitters with millions of lights. We stand on a hill and watch them sparkle. We stand by the fat river and watch the reflections in its dark waters. A man polishes my shoes so that they glisten too. In the centre, we are surrounded by Gucci, Prada, and Rolex. It seems like the whole world has come out to shop. We eat like we are rich, at banquets and in restaurants where the seats are covered in purple velvet. In the daytime, we shuffle past the sleeping Buddha and are carried with the crowds past the immortal beings carved into the ancient rocks. This is *da zu* 大足 county; 'big feet, ample, plenty'. There are certainly plenty of rock carvings, and plenty of tourists. This is a city of rolling hills, and trees; of women in heels and men in suits. A city where old friends sit around the table and drink late into the night.

Hong Kong 香港：

City of fusion; where the East meets the West. A fragrant harbour, where the seafood is always fresh, and on the island of Tai O, the fish are laid out to dry in the sun. In tiny cafes we sit on benches with strangers, eating macaroni and ham and drinking strong black tea, into which they pour condensed milk so that it turns slowly golden. In the countless winding streets, under countless neon signs, they sell blue crabs and miniature trees laden with oranges, helium balloons and designer shoes. Everyone wears a smile. The skyline is dotted with crosses that light up at night, and on the side of Victoria Peak someone has scrawled *'Jesus loves you;'* but on the outskirts, in the villages, we still find shrines to the ancient earth god. This is a city of multitudes. A conglomeration of myriad things. There's a bronze Buddha and a bronze Bruce Li, vast glass skyscrapers and tall thin palm trees, dirty old tin houses with gangly dogs asleep on their doorsteps, and bright new shopping malls with shiny floors and plush red carpets.

Chapter 11

Learning to Speak

学习说话

I tried to teach myself Chinese before I went to China. When I arrived, it came out of my mouth all wrong, and the people spoke it all wrong too. It didn't sound clear and slow and well-pronounced like the Chinese lady on my tape. They spoke the language fast and with many different accents. It sounded aggressive, like they were always angry with each other, and fierce, even when ordering a bowl of noodles. Aside from the basic *'hello'* and *'thanks'*, in those first weeks I got by with the most essential of phrases *wo ting bu dong* 我听不懂 *'I don't understand.'* To help me navigate the city, I had directions written down on paper, but sometimes the taxi drivers couldn't read. I spent a lot of time nodding my head or shaking it, shrugging my shoulders, or just smiling dumbly as I was cross-examined by curious fellow passengers on the bus or by waiters in a restaurant. Larger restaurants had pictures in their menus, so I had some inkling as to what I was ordering, but in smaller noodle and rice joints, you could only point at some squiggly characters and hope you got lucky. So, whilst learning the ropes of teaching, the bus routes of a new city, the best time to go to the supermarket, which dishes I liked, and whilst beginning to build relationships with students and colleagues and people who jumped out of bushes at me, I started to stumble up the lower slopes of the mammoth Mandarin Mountain.

This involved taking the tiny 704 bus to Xu Ni's flat, which was at the top of seven flights of stairs. I went once a week at first, and then, in the summer, twice, though it didn't make any difference to my language abilities. This was not Xu Ni's fault. It just happened that language study was difficult to do when my time was taken up with other things, and doing any homework was my last priority. So, I whiled away many hours sitting on the cellophane-covered sofa in Xu Ni's shadowy living room, trying hard to concentrate. Her toilet was special because it had its own fluffy seat cover, and there was no running water in the sink – just a plastic bowl with a little tepid water left standing in the basin. I felt proud when I remembered to say *wo gai zou le* 我该走了 *'I should go'* when I wanted to leave and when I thought of something other than *hai hao* 还好 *'Not bad'* when Xu Ni asked me how I was at the beginning of every class. During the summer months, Xu Ni took me out after class to eat at different hovels in the winding backstreets of a city 'village' destined to be demolished a few months later, though we didn't know it at the time. She introduced me to 'tofu brain' which floated in a bowl of lukewarm salty water, tasting strongly of old soya beans, and the best cold noodle vendor, whose wooden cart was propped up against a wall on the shady side of a street. We muddled along like this for a year, our lazy lessons only punctuated by the occasional excitement, like the time I was pickpocketed on the way there. Then Xu Ni became pregnant, and we moved to a little wicker table on her balcony, flooded by light, and our lessons became even sleepier in the warmth that enveloped the room. After Mao Mao was born during the summer holiday, lessons involved hushed tones while he slept or bizarre interactions with Xu Ni's mother as she held him in front of the mirror, crooning and laughing. Xu Ni's mother took up residence in their tiny flat for more than a year. A small lady with curly hair and narrow eyes, her Chinese was thickly coated by a strong regional accent, and she often reverted to the local dialect, which was incomprehensible to me.

Although I was able to speak to Xu Ni in Chinese, and she more often than not understood me, it was an entirely different matter speaking to anyone else. For some Chinese, as soon as they saw my white face, they were already convinced that I could not speak Chinese. Therefore, anything that came out of my mouth was impossible to understand even before it reached their ears. They might say, *"I don't speak English"* in Chinese, and I would think to myself, exasperated, *'But I'm speaking Chinese!'* I once attracted a whole crowd when buying porridge. The vendor could not understand my request for pumpkin porridge. Other customers got involved trying to help but were equally as bemused as the vendor. In the end, with an ever-growing circle of curious onlookers, I just pointed at a cup of red bean porridge and said, *"That one!"* Then I got out of there as fast as I could.

As an English teacher, I repeatedly told my students not to be afraid to make mistakes. Students at the English Corners we held would encourage one another to open their mouths and not be shy. A popular ditty went something like, *'Don't be shy, have a try, then you can speak like laowai.'*[13] Although I encouraged them all to speak and not to worry about always being accurate, I didn't always follow my own advice. I found it difficult to speak Chinese, especially when I was with other Westerners who spoke excellent Chinese and who were constantly praised by mutual friends and by beaming restaurant owners. I was told by a friend, in front of a group of Americans who were all fluent Mandarin speakers, that I spoke Chinese like a little girl, and another friend said *"like a five-year-old,"* which was probably being very generous.

Travelling across China one summer with two British friends, I was forced to use Chinese to help us get around. This led to some creative and interesting uses of the language, for example, asking a startled waitress, *jiaozi zai nar* 饺子在哪儿 *'Where are the dumplings?'* when we were looking for a dumpling restaurant.

With four tones (plus a neutral tone), it's very easy to say the wrong word by using the wrong tone. The tones also change depending on what word you are using and what word comes after it in a sentence. They also tend to blur in a sentence anyway, as people inflect to express emotion. And everybody talks fast, naturally. Tones are a minefield, particularly for someone who is probably tone-deaf, but then so is pronunciation.

---

13 Laowai is slang for foreigner.

There are many sounds we don't have in English and many sounds that sound similar but are not. It was complicated, and I was impatient. I had so much to say that I often couldn't be bothered to make sure the pronunciation and the tones were correct, which only slowed me down. So instead, I spoke the words with the nearest equivalent British sound and rushed on.

I continued bumbling along with my broken British Chinese, embarrassed by it but making excuses, until I went travelling one winter. It was while sitting around a fire in a small Dong village under a frosty sky of sharp stars that I felt a strong desire to be able to understand and communicate with Chinese people. Around the fire sat some elderly Dong women in their dark navy clothes, the fire flickering over their wizened faces as they chewed seeds and gossiped. I was so close to them physically and yet so far away that I could only watch them chuckling to themselves and gesticulating, wondering what they were talking about. Of course, these elderly women were speaking their own language, not Mandarin. And yet this kind of situation could be repeated a thousand times. I had sat with the families of friends multiple times as they chattered away around the dinner table, the relatives unable to speak English. In all their excitement, they easily forgot me; forgot I couldn't follow, and so I was isolated, unable to enter in. A male student had sat next to me on the school bus. He had a friend who was a Muslim. In broken English, he asked me about faith and with simple English and basic Chinese, I tried to tell him about Jesus. His name was Song, and I never saw him again. Not surprising in a university of over forty thousand students. To be able to speak Chinese would not only be extremely helpful in accomplishing everyday tasks, like getting my hair cut or explaining something to a workman, but it could open doors and enable a word of life to be spoken to someone.

Going to China was in some ways like becoming a child again. I often felt like a child when I was with groups of Chinese, only able to ask and answer simple questions, listening to them and trying to follow their conversations, picking up now and again on certain words and phrases. There was so much I didn't know; I was always only scraping the surface. Sometimes I was content to be the child, to let most of the conversation wash over me, and to spend much time alone in my own thoughts, even in the midst of a crowd. But at other times it was frustrating. Especially when I felt like a doll, passed around and patted. They took photos of me and praised my white skin or my green eyes. I was invited to events to be the foreign presence and raise the prestige by just being there – smile, shake hands, and nod. Maybe that's how the Queen used to feel! But, despite those feelings, which did grow less intense as both my Chinese and my confidence improved, I mostly felt a tremendous sense of privilege at being there – and valued – in a foreign land. And for that reason alone, I felt it worthwhile to at least attempt to learn the heart language of this people.

I began full-time language study in 2014. During those early days, I had to go back to the very beginning and try to master the same old sounds again. It was frustrating. One warm autumn afternoon, my window was open as I fretted over my books at my wobbly desk in my bedroom. I heard a voice in the small park outside, which drew my attention. A small Chinese girl was joyfully singing her ABCs. Her pronunciation was far from accurate, but she didn't seem to care. She was just happy to sing the same song over and over again. In that moment, I felt like God was saying to me, *'Be like that little girl;'* be happy to speak. It's not about producing the most accurate sounds, but about having joy in the process of learning. This was humbling. Perhaps language study for the missionary isn't just about learning to speak a foreign language; it's also about learning to be humble, to laugh at your mistakes, and to be like a child again, having joy in doing something simple, like reciting your ABCs under the shade of a magnolia tree.

Before I began full-time language study, God drew me to Jeremiah, chapter 32. Here, Jeremiah is told to buy a field. Jeremiah is confused by this command, as the Babylonians were laying siege to the city and it was about to be given into their hands. Why buy a field when he was about to go into exile and would not have the chance to enjoy it?

God told Jeremiah that the field was a guarantee that the people would eventually come back to the city, and there would once again be the purchasing of fields and land. I felt like language study was, in some ways, my 'field', the guarantee that I would be planted in the land, despite what might come. So, I learnt Chinese. And when I was at my most confident and was enjoying speaking the language and studying it, understanding and being understood, I came back to the UK, and I felt like I lost what I had just so recently gained. Why did God call me to study Chinese for two years when He then brought me back to this land, and for a long time, I didn't have the chance to use it? I didn't know. All I knew was that I had to trust Him. I had to trust Him when I chose to study Chinese, longing to be able to speak it and yet dreading the process. And then I had to trust Him when it seemed that even my 'field' was no longer mine to enjoy.

> *'Behold, I am the Lord, the God of all flesh. Is there anything too hard for Me? [...] I will bring them back to this place, and I will cause them to dwell safely [...] Yes, I will rejoice over them to do them good, and I will assuredly plant them in this land, with all My heart and with all My soul [...] And fields shall be bought in this land of which you say, "It is desolate"' (Jeremiah 32: verses 27, 37, 41, 43 NKJV).*

Chapter 12

Weeping in a BMW

自在宝马车里哭

I had no end of trouble with Chinese boys. They don't tell you about that when you sign up to go overseas! Apparently, I was just the *'right type,'* which meant that I shared some of the more traditional values that are still cherished by many in China, and I fitted the *feminine ideal'* of being gentle, quiet, and overly sensitive (as well as having white skin and double-fold eyelids). This ideal was evident in the way I walked. Grace walked with purpose in a determined manner. I walked like I needed someone to take care of me. And it seemed that there were plenty of enthusiastic Chinese boys willing to do just that. Therefore, I was plagued. Some of my experiences were funny, others quickly turned sour, and some just left a twinge of sadness as I encountered the loneliness, desperation, and emptiness of the young.

I met David at an English corner my students ran. About twelve students met on the ground floor of the library, standing in an atrium between the floor-to-ceiling glass windows and a kind of indoor shrubbery. There were no chairs, just a few metal benches screwed to the floor. Most of the students were typically shy and bashful, but there were, of course, as always, a few strong personalities who enjoyed speaking to the air at great length in English. We ended the evening with a few impromptu English folk dances. Then a small delegation walked me to the bus – something the students always did, as to *song* 送 'to see off' is an important part of Chinese culture.

Months later, David sent me a letter by the hand of one of my students. The letter contained a very long handwritten poem in Chinese about autumn and was signed by a *'Mr Wind.'* The student was sworn to secrecy, but it didn't take long for me to work out who it was from. At the English Corner, David had told me he loved writing poetry, and he also mentioned that his family name sounded similar to *feng* 风, the Chinese word for wind. Two years later, David Wind sent me another poem, along with a photograph of some dumplings he had made. This time the poem was in English:

> *Three-sentence love letter*
> *I mince my heart and enfold it into dumplings,*
> *For I want to know how does it taste to love you.*

In China, it seems that boys are still hopeless romantics. Chinese boys arrange candles in the shape of hearts outside the dormitories of their sweethearts. They carry the handbags of their girlfriends, even if they are pink and fluffy. They cycle across campus with their girlfriends sitting on the back racks of their wobbly bicycles, holding onto their skinny waists. They stand silently, without flinching, while their girlfriends throw violent tantrums in the middle of the street, sometimes even hitting them with their pink, fluffy handbags. In a country where there are nearly thirty-four million more males than females, there are a lot of single young men desperate for girlfriends and wives. On the campus of my university, an engineering school, there was a daily visual reminder of China's gross gender imbalance. When the bell rang to signify the end of class, the roads were flooded with students. Female students in their soft pastel shades were soon drowned in a sea of male students in their grungy greys, dark greens and navy blues. Male students often came to our English Corners looking for girlfriends. They were shy and socially awkward or lacked opportunities to meet girls anywhere else, having only two or three female students in their classes. Parents made sure their sons knew the importance of focusing solely on their studies while at university, but as soon as they graduated, the pressure was on to find a suitable spouse. As if, after years of ignoring girls to concentrate on memorising the rules of mathematical equations, their awkward son with dreams of Hollywood-style love and happy-ever-afters, could negotiate the complexities and survive the disappointments of a relationship with a real flesh and blood human being. I felt like these young Chinese males, whose glasses were permanently smeared and whose faded washing hung limply out of their windows to dry, still needed mothering, and I couldn't imagine that some of them, in a relatively short time, would be husbands.

Tiger was a male student full of starry-eyed notions of love. He was also a typical young Chinese who believed that *'hard to get'* was worth the chase, and that *'no'* meant *'try harder'* and *'don't give up.'* I met him once, very briefly, when he was talking to my friend. Then, out of the blue, that Christmas, he gave me a gift. After this came an invitation to see the giant lanterns in a park on a cold February night during Spring Festival. I went with another friend, and we met him there. Following this, I received a barrage of text messages from him daily, and always a *'good morning'* and *'good night'* text that continued incessantly for several months. In the summer, at the students' English Corner, Tiger showed up looking disgruntled and slightly harassed. I had long since stopped replying to his texts, having already told him that I was not interested. There were only a few students there that evening, now that it was close to exams. After an hour we ran out of things to say because everyone was tired, when suddenly Tiger came to life. He promptly picked up the conversation, choosing the next topic to be discussed as, rather specifically, one he entitled *'the most romantic thing that has ever happened to you.'* Before anyone else could make a start on the topic, Tiger began describing a story that happened one dark evening in a park covered in giant lanterns shaped like flowers and snakes; it being 2013, the year of the snake. In the park, he ordered some stinky tofu for a girl and, because she was holding the pot full of steaminess, plus a camera and a phone and other things (the tofu nearly ended up on the floor), he helped pull off her gloves. This was apparently the most romantic thing that had ever happened to him. Unfortunately, his pronunciation wasn't the best, so the word *'gloves'* sounded more like *'clothes'* and some of the students were quite startled by this (and had to be taken out of the room to recover). I may have added the bit about having to go out of the room. Actually, nobody left because they were all riveted to their seats. They all knew he was talking about me because of the way he was looking at me and the fact that I was shifting uncomfortably in my chair. The only person who wanted to get out of that room was me! After this embarrassing episode at the English Corner, there were a few lengthy emails exchanged. I pointed out that I'd actually only ever seen him four times: the brief initial hello, the brief encounter at Christmas, the evening at the park, and the awkward English Corner. This didn't seem to dissuade him. He replied, *'We just saw each other four times in total. It is hard for you to know me, not to speak to have feelings for me, you can see thousands of Chinese men like me every day, and I am just so small that you don't even notice. But you know what? I would still like you even if you were just another ordinary Chinese girl 'cause you already captured my heart.'* Thankfully, he was later sent to Europe as an exchange student, and so ended our correspondence.

In China, there is a strange mixing of the pragmatic with the idealised. For many, marriage is eventually no more than a business arrangement. By the end of their twenties, time is beginning to run out, and pressure from relatives intensifies. Unable to find their romantic ideal, many end up marrying someone who more or less fits the criteria that society sets. That is, someone from the same social class, educated to the same level, who has a good job and is financially secure. Unfortunately, pressure from relatives and society doesn't ease after marriage. Even at the wedding there are wishes of *zao sheng gui zi* 早生贵子 'Give birth to a son soon.' So, for most Chinese couples, children come along all too soon. It is astonishing how many Chinese can go from being single to married and having a child in such a relatively short space of time. Having a child pleases both sets of grandparents. The mother and father of the child then stay together for the sake of the child and, as is so often the case, everything is poured into that child because there is very little love, if any, between themselves. For some, a business arrangement is really quite suitable. Both parents can invest in their careers, feeling secure, and are able to socialise without their partners. Many Chinese men have extramarital affairs.

Many of my female friends were *sheng nv* 剩女 'leftover women'. The 'leftover' status is, of course, a much greater stigma for women than for men. My leftover friends were all in stable jobs, living in dormitories with other leftovers or renting a solitary room by themselves. At weekends, their concerned relatives arranged blind dates for them. They sat through countless dates in countless cafes, stirring countless coffees that had already gone cold. The verdict afterwards, when I asked, was always *"He talked about himself too much," "It felt like a long night,"* or *"There wasn't a spark."* These dates were more like interviews. Some anxious parents or controlling aunties even posted adverts about their single daughters and nieces in the park, meeting other anxious parents, swapping advice, and examining the other adverts that stated the credentials of single males in the city. My leftover friends dreaded the annual Spring Festival holiday where, like Christmas in the West, they were forced to make visits to relatives they didn't really like and, unlike Christmas in the West, they were compelled to sit through many conversations and cross-examinations where their elders discussed their singleness and asked pointed, personal questions. In China today, there are even agencies where you can hire a fake boyfriend or girlfriend to take home for the vacation and appease, for a time, your hyper-critical extended family and the ever-curious neighbours. For Christians, the pressure is even more intense. Chinese churches contain more women than men. Non-Christian parents often become angry and resentful if their daughters refuse to marry eligible men merely on the grounds that they do not share their faith. Indeed, many women buckle under such pressure and end up compromising, marrying a non-believer just to escape the constant accusations and complaints from their parents. Chinese parents can be tyrannical if they think they are acting in the best interests of their child. This often turns out to be in their own best interests.

At university, single students make light of their singleness, referring to themselves as *dan shen gou* 单身狗 'single dogs.' For them, the more intense pressure is yet to come. University provides a four-year lull sandwiched between the pressure and discipline of their childhood, where they worked hard studying in order to take the entrance examination and enter a good university, and post-graduation, when the pressure resumes and they are expected to find a good job, a suitable spouse, and then start a family. For many young students, the new sense of freedom and the relaxing of parental control during university life, at first perhaps wonderful, soon leads to feelings of listlessness and depression. Many do not know how to use their time or how to study independently because previously their free time had been filled for them with extra classes in Olympic maths and violin, and 'studying' just meant memorising the textbook and everything the teacher said. Many are unable to form deep and lasting relationships because previously their friendships had been restricted to the classroom or online forums, and there was never much time for socialising anyway. Chinese students often open up to their foreign teachers and friends because they are unable to share deeper feelings of depression and disappointment, their fears for the future, and their fears of failure with their Chinese peers. To share such things with older Chinese relatives is nigh on impossible. The most common feelings that were shared with me were the feelings of being trapped, of not being in control of their future, of being stuck in the system, and of being unable to truly trust anyone.

When talking to Chinese female students about what they look for in the opposite sex, the answer often comes back as *gao fu shuai* 高富帅 'tall, rich, handsome', which is, of course, half-jokingly said. However, there is a very real tendency among Chinese women to focus on wealth when looking for a potential partner. In China, there is such a thing as the bride price—a hangover from pre-Communist times that is still going strong today. The bride price is usually a certain amount of money that the groom's family pays to the bride's, so that, in a sense, they are 'buying' the bride out of her family. In the recent past, the bride price might have been furniture or a refrigerator; at one time just a thermos flask would have been sufficient. But today, the stakes are getting higher. In some areas, the bride price can reach the equivalent of twelve thousand pounds in cash, and the groom is also often expected to have a flat with decent furniture, and sometimes even a car as well. In rural places, where women are significantly outnumbered by men and therefore in high demand, women can ask for what they like. Marriage customs in these places have been flipped upside down; single men are now on the market, and women are the consumers. These countryside men and involuntary bachelors are often nicknamed *'bare branches.'* Villages that contain a large number of such men are called *'bare branch villages.'* In such places—and indeed across China—women can afford to set the bar high when looking for a spouse. China is becoming more and more materialistic, and many younger people seem driven only by the pursuit of money and material comforts. An example of this is Ma Nuo, who made famous the phrase *'I'd rather weep in a BMW than laugh on a bicycle'* on a dating show when invited by a male contestant to ride a bicycle with him. Although she may have been using this phrase in a creative way to reject the unwanted suitor, the phrase seems to reflect an attitude prevalent among China's youth and a shallowness I encountered time and time again when young Chinese told me their goal for the future was to make lots of money.

Before I went to China, I was looking forward to being in a culture where there was less emphasis put on looking a certain way. I somehow imagined that Chinese women and culture were less concerned with make-up and fashion and air-brushed models. So, I was shocked to discover that the emphasis on physical appearance was ten times more intense. Most of my female friends, already matchstick thin or at least on the smaller end of what is regarded as 'average' in the UK, were on diets. They also complained about being *'black'* by which they meant tanned. In China, thin and white is in. Social media buzzed periodically with different beauty challenges through which Chinese girls determined whether they were thin enough or had the perfect Chinese body. There was the A4 waist challenge (if a vertical piece of paper covered your waist, your waist was small enough) and the belly button challenge (if you could twist your arm around your back to touch your belly button, your bones were small enough). There was also the iPhone 6 challenge: if your phone covers both your knees when laid horizontally across (the phone is less than five and a half inches in height) then you are well on your way to fitting into the small bones, tiny waist, and flat-bottomed body ideal that Chinese culture is obsessed with. As a Westerner shopping in China, I always ended up having to buy the XXL size (if they stocked it). When I returned a denim skirt once because it was too small, the shop owner found it hilarious and declared to the shop that I had a belly! In a Chinese airport, the security officer who frisked me asked me how many months pregnant I was. Punan, the Chinese auntie in charge of our building, as I mentioned earlier, never had any qualms telling me I'd put on weight, and one middle-aged mother at our English Corner once patted my stomach and told me it was unsightly. Chinese are not shy when it comes to noticing and commenting on physical features that they regard as not nice-looking. I'll always remember the time when a student greeted a German with the words, *"Your nose is big."* Thankfully, the man took it on the chin and responded with, *"Well, it's the one I was born with."*

Chapter 13

Double Happiness

囍

Chinese weddings are normally raucous affairs and no two weddings are alike. Customs and traditions differ from province to province and from village to village within each province. Sue took us to a wedding in her village. We stayed overnight in her family's second house (the first house was where the family lived – a small brick building with hens in the front yard and goats out the back). Sue's second house was newly built and not yet lived in. Her family seemed to prefer the hard dirt floor of the older one, with its cramped conditions, worn-out furniture, and posters from years gone by still tacked to the walls, to the new house, which was spacious and white and clean with its protective plastic film peeling off the doors. We got up really early and made our way down the dirt track to the bride's house. She was a robust country girl with a round face and thick brown hair. It was early spring, and the day was dry and bright though there was a chill in the air. Sue was the bridesmaid, though she just wore ordinary clothes. Her duties seemed to involve ordering people around, reassuring the bride, and helping her to heavily powder her face. We hovered around the bride's bedroom as she squeezed herself into a white wedding dress, pulled on long white gloves and then sat down in the centre of her bed, the skirt of her dress billowing out, forming a protective netting all around her and giving her the appearance of a large swan. Her dress was probably second-hand, which was just as well because the sequin bodice later tore away from the skirt, and she ripped the dress in several places, including a sleeve. This didn't matter though because she already had her wedding photos proudly displayed in varying sizes around her bedroom, as Chinese couples take their wedding photographs pre-wedding, sometimes months before the actual ceremony. Around this bride's bedroom were photographs of her and her husband-to-be in traditional red qipaos and suits, as well as cowboy outfits and Mao-era green military uniforms. In her room, she also had a pair of red stiletto shoes, which Sue promptly hid within and then locked the door. We all sat down to wait.

It wasn't long before we heard an unruly ruckus outside as the groom and several of his male friends arrived. After yelling and hammering on the door to no avail, they then attempted to break it down, with the women within meanwhile, yelling back at them in violent Chinese, refusing them entry. There was lots of scuffling and shouting while the bride excitedly jumped up and down on the bed, until the windows gave in as some of the men took them apart from the outside. In all the commotion, we just looked on and tried to stay out of the way of crumbling mortar and crushing bodies. Eventually, having pulled the window frames off the wall, the men were allowed entry into the room (through the usual point of entry—the door) after slipping red envelopes filled with cash under it. When Sue decided the amount of money was sufficient, she opened the door. The groom, dressed in a dark suit with a thick red sash draped over his shoulder and across his chest, then proceeded to pull the bedroom apart in a desperate and noisy attempt to find the red shoes. Having found them under a pillow and behind a chair, he hunkered down on his knees and pushed the red shoes onto the stout feet of his beloved. The ever-increasing crowd of neighbours, relatives, and other well-wishers that were standing outside during this process all squeezed into the small room so that it was filled to the brim with hoots of laughter as jokes were bandied back and forth. Small bowls were passed to the bride and groom, and they clumsily fed each other the dumplings inside, much to the amusement of the onlookers.

After all this noise and merriment, a long procession of cars took the bride (and everyone else) to the groom's village. In front of the procession, an open truck slowly bounced along, with six short swarthy men sitting within, banging cymbals together and hitting large red drums to scare off evil spirits. We followed along at a snail's pace, the driver intermittently honking his horn to add to the chaos. When we arrived at the groom's front yard, an explosion of firecrackers greeted us, and we were lost for some time, in thick clouds of smoke. Outside the yard, the Master of Ceremonies was ready, dressed in a red mandarin collared shirt and holding a loudspeaker in his hand. He was a small man with a merry, moonlike face who rocked back and forth on the balls of his feet and laughed hilariously at everything. The villagers welcomed the bride with a clownish dance; some of them dressed in a clownish way, and others banged together more cymbals and made even more noise. The ceremony took place in the front yard, but to get inside, where many of the guests sat waiting, the bride had to force her way past the groom and his male friends, who stood barring the way. Now it was the bride's turn to shove and hit and pull and eventually elbow her way through the human barrier, destroying her dress in the process. The ceremony itself involved the Master of Ceremonies chortling and teasing the newlyweds as he bounced up and down on the red carpet that covered the dirt floor of the yard and led them slowly through a set of rituals that included bowing to each set of parents, to each other, and then to the earth. Etiquette and formalities over, the most important part of the wedding followed – the part that all the guests were secretly waiting for – the banquet. Tables were pulled out, benches pulled up, and dishes seamlessly rolled out of the house. There were so many that the plates ran out, and an impromptu washing-up team sprang up in one corner of the yard, complete with a hose and a great volume of bubbles. As token foreigners, my friend and I were called on to do our bit and provide some entertainment. We decided to add some British solemnity to the preceding events by reading 1 Corinthians 13, translated by Sue. Like most Chinese audiences, our audience didn't appear to be paying the slightest bit of attention to our eloquent and dignified reading. Whether at a speech contest or a cinema, a wedding or a musical performance, members of a Chinese audience will fidget, get up repeatedly for no apparent reason, use their phones to make a call, and continue a conversation with their friend two rows in front of them. This wedding audience was even worse than the average. They all continued to talk while we read, so we did our best to shout into the microphones, hoping our voices might be heard over the general din they were making.

Katy took me to a wedding in her old village, where the groom's house was a cave and the village's toilets consisted of two small yellow brick buildings, big enough for one person to crouch in, a little way down the dusty hill, next to the goats and donkeys. A large tent was erected for the banquet, and a catering team arrived to prepare the food in a special wooden van. The bride wore black trousers and a thick white coat. The only thing that identified her as the bride was a red sash across her chest. Though it was winter the sun shone strongly, and its light bounced off the horns, gongs, and pipes of a brass band that played in front of the cave dwelling. The wedding banquet here was a succession of dishes and meals that continued throughout the day. We ate buckwheat noodles when we arrived and then periodically made our way back to the tent at different intervals to fill up on other dishes. At one point, a mass of red envelopes were exchanged at a table surrounded by a crowd of onlookers who jeered, clapped and called out. The wedding lasted the whole day. Wandering around with Katy's little cousin, we spent some time in the living room where a bunch of men from the village sat around smoking and drinking loose tea in polystyrene cups while hotly debating something. Things turned political, if they hadn't already, when one man asked where I was from and then started talking about Hong Kong and the British. While a debate began in the room over whether the British occupation of Hong Kong had turned out to be good or evil, the small cousin and I slipped out of the room and down the hill to poke a donkey.

Katherine and Lizzie's weddings were completely different affairs. Both took place in the city, beginning in hotel rooms where the bride and her friends waited for the groom to arrive. At both of these weddings, the groom was allowed into the room only after he had satisfied the bridesmaids by providing enough red envelopes and by answering some questions about the bride or doing some challenges. For Lizzie's husband, this included saying some tongue twisters in English. The poor man couldn't speak a word. From the hotel, Katherine and her guests were driven to another venue for the ceremony, which was a Christian one, complete with a small choir from her local church. Katherine's wedding reflected more of a Western style, with her dad, who looked rather like Barak Obama, albeit in a Chinese way, walking her down the aisle. There was a sermon from her pastor and, except for the obligatory firecrackers, the whole thing was altogether a more solemn and quiet affair. Instead of bowing, the bride and groom served their parents tea to express their gratitude. The banquet that followed the ceremony was still very elaborate, but unlike most wedding banquets, there was no potent rice alcohol on the tables, so no one got drunk when toasting the newlyweds. Instead, there was a rather long queue for the toilet as the afternoon wore on and all the Sprite ran out.

Lizzie's wedding was luxurious. It began in a private hotel for government officials, surrounded by beautiful grounds, the lawn freshly mowed, with a tranquil lake in the centre encircled by willows. Then a procession of vehicles took us to the apartment where Lizzie would live with her husband. Everything in it was new and clean and shiny. I sat on her immaculate smooth sofa and was offered seeds and small cakes like puffs of air on a gleaming tray. Another procession of vehicles took us to yet another grand hotel. Lizzie changed her dress (she changed four times throughout the day), and the ceremony began in a huge reception room with chandeliers and a deep red carpet that was so thick your shoes sank several inches into it. We sat on tables around a platform, rather like a catwalk, covered with white silk and pink flowers. On a large screen, a video played on a loop, showing pictures of the couple. Throughout the afternoon many speeches were given by prominent and prestigious individuals. Lizzie's cousin sang a song, a spotlight hovering over him and highlighting the beads of sweat on his brow. The food at this banquet was exotic and expensive – lobster and duck, whole fish and scallops, sea cucumbers and sea snails. In contrast to the abundance on display, Lizzie looked anorexic, and although she smiled and chatted, greeted the guests and shouted orders at the photographer, she seemed tense and on edge, like she might crack at any moment. Not surprising with the size of her wedding. Even my friend and I began to crumble at our table. We took a taxi home, and I went and ordered a Chinese hamburger.

Chapter 14

Small Stones

小小的石头

I never knew how to hold a baby until a Chinese girl took me to the baby home and showed me. I don't know why I kept going every week with that girl and then eventually on my own. At first, it was, if I'm honest, boring. The room was always hot, and the babies always cried. It was tiring to try to amuse them, shaking rattles or singing songs. They were heavy in my arms and smelt of milk powder and sweat. Then I was asked to take the babies swimming. At first, three of us went with three of the children; one was already about three, and the other two were toddlers. We pushed the children in prams and pushchairs, their wheels squeaking, across wide roads heavy with traffic, and along streets hazy with heat and pollution. The pool itself might have been cool if the ceiling hadn't been glass. I continued to visit the children during the week, taking them out to the park with an auntie if the weather was good and they didn't have runny noses. These children were constantly ill. I bumped a baby's head on the slide and he bawled. Grace said she heard a baby crying somewhere outside. *"That was my fault,"* I said. I really felt overwhelmed and out of my depth with these small children. I was in no way, shape or form, fit – or inclined – to become a 'nursemaid.' This was not what I came to China to do, so when Sun, the man in charge of the home, said I was an answer to his prayer to look after these little ones, I was somewhat dubious.

My Chinese vocabulary grew in all things connected with babies – milk powder and nappies, simple commands like *'Blow bubbles!'* and nursery rhymes about tigers with one ear and no tail. I spent most of my volunteering time at the second baby home. It began to grow as they were allowed to bring more babies out of the state orphanages. As children were adopted, others took their place. By the end of two years volunteering there, we had grown from three children to eleven, and the first home had doubled in size too. When a baby arrived from the state orphanage, you could tell where they had come from. When Peter arrived, he was probably ten months old. He shrank from being touched and was content just to lie on his back staring at the ceiling. But as the weeks and months rolled by, this little boy with Down syndrome began to grow and thrive. He got used to cuddles, and he loved music and songs. When I left, he could sit up unaided and stand, holding onto the fence of the plastic playpen.

The aunties who worked with the babies were mostly middle-aged women from the city or surrounding countryside. Most of them were Christians, willing to work for a charity[14] for a much smaller wage than they might get elsewhere. They worked hard changing nappies and feeding babies until, hopefully, a forever family came to take away each child – forever – to America or Italy, Spain, and sometimes, though more rarely, to other cities in China. It seemed, in some ways, a bittersweet job and one overlooked by many. Those simple women, most of them uneducated, spent their hours caring for little ones who would not remember them in years to come after they ended up scattered across the world. God, however, saw each one and saw the hours spent and the hearts that both grieved and rejoiced at each parting. This was a truly sacrificial work.

At Spring Festival, the staff were depleted somewhat as most of the aunties took time away to visit relatives. During this time, I went every afternoon and stayed with the children while the remaining aunties went out for dinner. While they were out, I had control of eleven babies and

---

14 Non-governmental organisation

toddlers – a small army. Most of them were old enough to understand simple commands; some were beginning to play make-believe; and a few were starting to speak. Four of the children had shoes with squeaks inside, and they enjoyed marching excitedly up and down the flat, filling the whole place with their high-pitched, squeaky footsteps. The squeaks were eventually pulled out, and the four of them were surprised to find their footsteps suddenly silent.

All of the children had disabilities: Down syndrome, dwarfism, cleft palate and cleft lip, heart defects, hermaphroditism, and hearing defects. There were always more boys than girls. Sometimes a child with quite severe problems came to the home, like Star, a very small girl with cerebral palsy who was too weak to sit up and who wriggled out of your arms when held. Star spent a lot of time lying alone on the mat. She struggled to eat too, spitting out the food she was given and hence growing thinner and weaker. When a volunteer came from South Africa, she took a special interest in Star. She saw her every day and sometimes took her home for the night. Over this period, Star gradually began to develop. She would laugh whenever she saw that lady. When that lady left, there was a time when a blonde-haired girl came to visit, and Star rolled all across the mats to her feet, perhaps mistaking her for her South African friend because of the colour and length of her hair.

Taking the children out, we got lots of stares. When I used to pick up one little boy, grandmas and aunties often wandered over to look at us. *"Is he yours?"* they'd ask. *"Yang wa wa"* 洋娃娃 'foreign baby,' they'd say to each other, squeezing his chubby Chinese cheeks. The Chinese love children. They love to give advice about childcare and to poke, cuddle, and pass around any babies they come across like they are small, squishy parcels. Most young children in China are raised by their grandmas whilst their parents work long hours. Every day you can spot grandmas taking their grandchildren out for a stroll in the neighbourhood or a walk in the park, ambling along in their baggy patterned trousers and slippers, the child on a rein or squatting down somewhere for a wee.

Walking through residential areas and local communities, one would think the population of China was predominantly made up of babies and the elderly. As an only child, many children have the attention of both sets of grandparents as well as their parents. This is known as the '*4-2-1 syndrome*' – four grandparents, two parents, one child. As China's middle and upper-class urbanites increasingly have more cash to splash, this attention and extravagance sometimes results in one very spoilt child. Hence, these pampered children have earned the nickname '*Little Emperors.*' As these children grow older, one wonders what will they be like? What will the effects of the 'Little Emperor Syndrome' entail for China? Chinese culture has been, for thousands of years, a collective culture in which children must think of their families before themselves, sacrificing their independence and their own desires for the wishes of their parents and the honour of their families. This ancient Confucian value is referred to as '*filial piety.*' Perhaps the end of filial piety is now in sight? Will subsequent generations of indulged and self-focused children cause this ancient collective culture to turn in on itself? I met some older 'Little Empresses' at university. In some ways, they seemed more 'Western' in their focus on themselves. Their interests included spending money, buying clothes, going to fancy restaurants, and taking photos of the dishes they ate, the food growing cold as they moved cutlery around to get the best angle in the best light. The photograph always got edited and filtered before being uploaded to social media. Selfie sticks followed these people everywhere they went.

Everything you've ever heard about China is probably true at some point in its long history or in some part of its vast land, or for someone among its teeming millions. For every Little Emperor in the city, there are probably ten more children in the countryside who are more like Mia or June. Born secretly into families that already had children, they were given away to other relatives, or even strangers, to raise. Some of them were eventually sent back to their parents' home when they were older, though they were, in effect, little more than strangers in their own family. Neighbours were told that the child who had come to stay was a cousin or a niece from far away. The neighbours pretended to buy the story. Perhaps *'Little Emperor Syndrome'* also serves to highlight the ever-increasing gap between China's rich and poor?

I took friends and students with me to volunteer at the baby home. For most, it was the first time they'd ever taken part in voluntary work and also the first time they'd encountered an orphan or held a child with disabilities. They were often touched and sent me messages like the following: *'Thank you so much. I don't know how to say it. You went to charity and played with children; I was shocked because I saw light from you. You made me know what is big love.'* A friend once even said, "*Wow! You are just like Yesu* 耶稣 *[Jesus]*." She didn't know what that meant to me. However, it was a bit of a balancing act to bring volunteers to the charity. On the one hand, they desperately needed volunteers to play with the children or take them out, and yet, too many volunteers could draw too much attention and create other problems.

Sometimes there were lockdowns, due to illness amongst the children, or for other reasons. Occasionally, children were taken back by the authorities to state orphanages. Things would change very quickly in China and the work came up against all manner of obstacles. Sometimes it seemed there was no end to these, as one trying circumstance was followed by another. There were five months when no one was allowed to visit the children because they had foot and mouth disease and were quarantined. This was normal life in China and it demanded both faith and courage. There were so many things outside of our control, so many things that were uncertain, so much we didn't know from moment to moment. We didn't know how things would work out. These circumstances lent themselves to prayerfulness, and I learnt much about my posture before God, a never-ending lesson of coming back to a place of trust.

Despite my reluctant start, these children quickly and easily stole my heart. Xiao Bo was always the first to stride over and claim my lap. Mei was OCD in the way she ordered bricks by colour and size. Ceorge always had a tantrum after dinner because he wanted more food. Pan

Pan had the cheekiest smile, and Xiao Yu caused the most mischief, seizing toys from the others. There were only eleven children, rescued from the many hundreds in the institutions of that city, the many thousands across the country. They were just the tip of the iceberg, just the small stones at the bottom of a mighty mountain, but, as the Chinese proverb says, the person who removes a mountain must begin by carrying away small stones.

Chapter 15

Of Loss
丢去的

The first thing I noticed was my hair. The Chinese hairdresser noticed it too and told Sue that I should be careful. A year later, in the UK during the summer, our family hairdresser told me my hair was thinning. I felt unwell hearing those words; I was shocked, although I had known for some time that my ponytail was getting smaller. I went to my doctor and, after a few tests in which nothing untoward was flagged up, he told me to eat healthily and do plenty of exercise. I went back to China for my fourth year, and things started to get much worse.

Mia decided to help me. Mia was one of those direct and outspoken Chinese, unafraid to tell you if your clothes were ugly or your thighs too large. She noticed my hair immediately. She took me to a Chinese medicine doctor who felt my pulse, observed my tongue, and asked me some very private questions in front of a shop crammed full of curious patients, all leaning in on the conversation. *Qi xu* 气虚 was his verdict – a deficiency of qi (vital energy) and the cure was contained in several plastic bags of liquid herbs that I had to heat up every morning. The medicine was thick and red, a bitter substance that tasted like hot blood and moved slowly down my throat like molten liquid. It revived me for a time, probably through the ordeal of drinking it, but after two weeks, the bags were all used up, and I didn't go back to the doctor because the bus ride to his shop took more than an hour and Mia herself was falling apart. She lost another job, and her already fragile mental health continued to splinter. She acted strangely, walking miles in the snow to see me when she could have taken the bus, arriving wild-eyed with her hair wet and tangled. She wouldn't eat very much, and yet when I was out, she ate most of the food in my house. She took showers in the middle of the night and spent hours in the bathroom. Though we were both up to our waists in our own problems, we blindly floundered around trying to help each other. Mia insisted I eat nutritious food, which, in her opinion, meant black sesame porridge, milk, nuts and red dates. We bought grains and nuts from a peddler who stood in the shadows on the corner of the street at dusk – a tall man who wore a Russian hat and a long black trench coat. His machine was like an old cement mixer, and with much spluttering and noise, it ground up grains into a fine powder that could be used to make a porridge. That year I ate more healthily than I'd ever eaten before, but perhaps it was too late to make any difference.

As my hair continued to fall out, I went through periods of stoicism, resigned to the fact that I might lose my hair, and then I went through periods of feeling extremely distressed, almost like my very existence was being threatened. I now recognise this as a trauma response. I felt overwhelmed and powerless, knowing my health was beginning to crumble, yet I never thought about telling anyone about it. At those times I wrote down verses like the following: *'He has fenced up my way so that I cannot pass; and He has set darkness in my paths. He has stripped me of my glory and taken the crown from my head' (Job 19:8-9).* If my hair was my glory, then that glory was slowly being stripped away from me. At that time, I was seeking the Lord about moving to another city to start a new work, and it seemed like doors were opening rather quickly. Yet later, I would not be able to pass through them.

I had a childhood fear that I would lose my hair. This may have been fuelled by watching a documentary about children with cancer and not fully understanding that the children on the screen were sick. There was a girl in my primary school who came to school wearing a hat because she had leukaemia and her hair had fallen out. Even my favourite TV show had an episode in which the main character was cursed, and that curse made her hair fall out. I was so frightened one night that I couldn't sleep, not until my dad had prayed with me. Perhaps old fears that still lurk in our hearts, even those from our long-forgotten childhood, have to be dragged out into the light to be completely destroyed if we are to go on, to thrive, and to flourish. Our unspoken brokenness needs to eventually be given words. God has a perfect time and way to bring out and deal with the half-forgotten things we've buried, and sometimes the only way to conquer our fears is to be forced to face them. When that old fear became real and I was paralysed in response to it, I eventually discovered, behind it and through it, the tenderness of a God whose heart for us is to make us whole.

Not only did I lose my hair, but I also lost my health. I started to have diarrhoea, often straight after I had eaten, sometimes repeatedly. I assumed I had a fast metabolism. Then there was the bloating that sometimes made me look pregnant. I thought I had put on some serious weight, so I tried to lose a little. The blind masseur who gave me a massage in his shop above the dumpling restaurant told me my neck was the worst he'd ever felt and that I needed to do some exercise. It was true – my neck was stiff and painful. He recommended swimming. I disliked swimming but was keen to follow his advice, so I set off for the swimming pool on my bicycle. It was mid-June, and the streets were like an oven. At noon, the streets were empty except for a few old men sitting in shady corners. The pool, however, was packed. It was standing room only in the water, which had turned a dirty beige colour, and the whole pool smelt of bodies and steam. People lounged on plastic chairs around the side of the pool, eating grapes, crisps, and spicy bean curd, the condensation from the glass ceiling dripping slowly onto their heads. The tiny changing room was crammed full of semi-naked bodies. I stuck it out in the pool for about thirty minutes, then cycled back to my flat under clouds of stifling smog. I thought I'd leave swimming until I came home in the summer.

Foot massage is extremely popular in China, and small clinics can be found almost on every street. You didn't need to book; just walk straight in. Hot water was poured into bamboo buckets in which bags of herbs floated, flavouring the water and giving it a strong steamy fragrance. While you soaked your feet, the masseur massaged your neck and back. After this, he trimmed your toenails and scraped the dead skin off your heels with a blade, followed by a massage with cream. Throughout this process, the masseur, from his knowledge of reflexology and intimate acquaintance with your feet, delighted in telling you about your health. Every foot masseur I went to during this period told me I had a problem with my digestion. Just from massaging my feet, they could tell that something was wrong. I used to think that reflexology hadn't a foot to stand on and that Chinese Traditional Medicine was medical quackery. I'm not so sure what to think now. Maybe it's another case of *'There are more things in heaven and earth, Horatio, than are dreamt of in your philosophy.'*

That summer the heat was almost unbearable. I was covered in prickly heat rash that itched for weeks. A friend took me and her daughter to the zoo to escape the heat. Outside the zoo they were selling tiny white rabbits in pink cages. It was so hot that the air was shimmering and people said you could cook an egg on the pavement. The zoo had a safari park and as we took the bus around it, my friend told me the story of a father and son who had both met a tragic end in the park a few years before. The son had just passed his entrance exam to university and to celebrate, his proud dad decided to take him to the zoo. Unable to afford the entrance ticket, they climbed over the fence instead, right into the lion enclosure where they were both attacked and killed by lions. I was relieved that my friend's seven-year-old daughter was unable to follow her mother's rapid English. It put a bit of a damper on things. The zoo was a miserable place. Skinny wolves lay in the shadows of their cages, tongues lolling out, a sad looking elephant sprayed dust over his skin in an attempt to cool down, and a leopard ran in circles around his cage, mad and panting. It was too hot to eat lunch so we sucked ice lollies instead.

That summer, lots of people seemed to be leaving. It was my last summer too, though I didn't know it at the time. There were ceremonies to attend and leaving parties, and countless goodbye meals. The day before I left China for the long summer holiday, I wrote down the following: *'But God is faithful [to His Word and to His compassionate nature], and He [can be trusted] not to let you be tempted and tried and assayed beyond your ability and strength of resistance and power to endure, but with the temptation He will [always] also provide the way out (means of escape to a landing place), that you may be capable and strong and powerful to bear up under it patiently' (1 Corinthians 10:13 AMP)*. Feeling overwhelmed and weak, I cried out to the Lord for rest and healing. He graciously answered my prayer by taking me home and keeping me there. I had booked a return ticket home despite having a strong feeling that I should only buy a single one. I wanted rest and healing, but I also wanted to get back to China as soon as possible. I thought the summer holiday would be sufficient time to get well, but God took much longer.

Chapter 16

Beyond Myself

超越老我

During my last two years in China, God gave me more opportunities to work with children with special needs. He gave me a heart for them, though at the same time He also began to show me how far short I fell in being able to truly love others. I came to the realisation that it was always myself that kept me from really loving people. If I could somehow forget myself, I would really be able to love without hindrance or without restraint. I was led to pray that God would take me beyond myself.

The children I worked with were orphans. In some ways, China is full of orphans, both literal and spiritual. To the young women I befriended, many of whom had mental health problems, and to the children, I felt almost like a mother. When I believed, in my last year, that God was leading me into working with an orphanage and a training school that cared for children with disabilities, I was willing to go, although I felt it was rather beyond myself and my skill set. A verse that continued to claim my attention during those years was Habakkuk 2:3: *'For the vision is yet for an appointed time and it hastens to the end [fulfilment]; it will not deceive or disappoint. Though it tarry, wait [earnestly] for it, because it will surely come; it will not be behindhand on its appointed day'* (AMP). A month before I left China, I read those verses again, and in my diary I underlined a quote from a writer writing on that passage: *'Sometimes God says, wait! Stop working to make things happen before their time!'*

In those last years, I often prayed that God would make me totally dependent on Him. I was more and more aware that without Him I could do nothing. I also regularly prayed that God would unlock me. I felt like I was, in some ways, like the garden in the book '*The Secret Garden.*' That garden is hidden behind high walls, kept closed for many years. When some children discover the garden, they assume that it is dead, but after pulling up weeds and raking away dead leaves, when spring comes buds begin to sprout, and life that was long hidden is uncovered and allowed to bloom. Eventually, the garden's gates are thrown open as the healing influence of the beautiful garden changes the hearts and lives of those who walk within it. I knew I had life and goodness within me, sown there by His hand, but I was locked up just like that garden, yearning to grow and to open up to others, yet unable to free myself.

God answered these prayers in ways I didn't expect. On arriving home, my health deteriorated quite rapidly. It was like being hit with a ton of bricks. The diarrhoea was incessant and often unexpected. The anxiety it created gradually grew over the months, affecting everything that I had taken for granted. I was used to being independent, travelling by myself to interesting places, but now I was anxious just walking through the town. I was unable to eat, I couldn't go to a restaurant or to the cinema without considerable stress, and I wasn't even able to sit down with my family and watch TV, let alone sink comfortably into a chair. I was constantly on edge and unable to relax. If people talked to me, I couldn't concentrate on what they were saying. My hypervigilant mind was buzzing with my own anxious thoughts. I went to church desperate to hear God speak to me, to give me a Word that I could hold onto that would make sense of what was happening to me and give me some hope, though I sat through the service with my palms soaked in sweat. It was like God had removed everything that I depended on and loved. I was left fragile and trembling, disconnected from the people around me, and unable to feel safe in my body. This I can now name as a maladaptive stress response – in other words, the body's response to trauma in which the nervous system gets stuck. I was to be stuck in collapse, in a 'freeze' survival mode, for over seven years.

In those early months, I felt like I was groping through the darkness, seeking a diagnosis that consistently avoided me and hoping that once found, recovery would be quick and easy. I went through a series of hopes followed by bitter disappointments, of what Wilda Mathews described as *'a sudden fluttering of [my] hearts' wings'* [that] *'soared high for a short spin, only to make a forced landing in more mud.'*[15] Diagnoses and treatments did come, and many of them from many different quarters (including parasites, candida and post-viral M.E. and 'discovered' by doctors, a chiropractor, and an orthodontist!), but none of the diagnoses or treatments gave me the complete healing I expected. The treatment I received for the official diagnosis of lymphocytic colitis was muddled up by miscommunication with the hospital, so I didn't receive the correct dosage at the right time. Hope deferred makes the heart sick. Through all these disappointments, I felt my spirit was slowly being worn down. I was lost and completely helpless; it seemed that no-one had answers, or rather, that everyone had a different answer, and no matter how hard I tried to follow all these 'leads' not one of them led me out to green pastures. There was only ever a further entanglement and confusion. I was completely isolated and at war with my body.

Through this, God took away my reliance on other people. I was somehow unable to express myself or what I was going through to others, so even if they asked or sought to draw alongside me, there was an invisible barrier between my heart and theirs. I was closed off to God alone, unable to connect with or share my experience and heartache with anyone. This was God's doing too, for everything that comes to us comes from His hand.

For seven months, I was on a highly restrictive diet under the guidance of a herbalist. This diet made me weaker and more anxious than ever. On less than half the calories I needed every day, I had very little energy

---

15 Quoted in *'Green Leaf in Drought'* by Isobel Kuhn, p. 48

and couldn't sleep at night. Every day I felt like I was on the edge of disaster, walking along a narrow ridge that either side dropped down into great empty chasms. I went through a constant cycle of crying out to God in despair, then hearing God speak and believing Him, then crying out to Him again. It was endless and exhausting. He was all I had at that time and the only One I was able to fully depend on, though in my frailty and fear I often doubted Him and viewed my present difficulties and challenges with both immense fear and intense shame.

Throughout this time, I still held all the promises of God in my heart – promises I felt He'd given to me, to 'plant' me in the land of China. As I encountered more setbacks, it seemed more impossible that I would go back. There was a huge gap between where I was and where I longed to be, and I didn't know how to cross it. For a long time, I tried to gain control of my situation and speed my recovery myself, through diets and supplements, over-the-phone counselling, and endless trawling through internet forums. I tried to help myself and find my own way out. This became an addiction that lasted for years, and cost me greatly, both financially, but also by consuming my energy. It also displayed a lack of trust in the Lord and reliance on Him, for He has promised to always lead us: *'I will teach you and tell you the way to go and how to get there; and I will give you good counsel and I will watch over you'* (Psalm 32:8 VOICE).

Yet I can be gentle with myself now, something I am slowly learning, and acknowledge that though struggling and striving was not what God wanted for me, the desire in my heart – the hope and faith I had – that wholeness and healing was coming was not wrong in itself. I never gave up. Like the woman with the issue of blood who spent all her money on physicians and yet grew worse, I also kept believing and hoping and trying to move forward, trying to discern God's voice in it all.

In the end, I had to (repeatedly) acknowledge my total lack of control and powerlessness and come back to a place of quiet trust and waiting. Several times I had to submit – to willingly give up my hope of a return to China and my obsession with getting well. God had already shown me that I was making idols of both of these things, honing in on them so that they were all I thought about; making them so big in my mind that I couldn't see beyond them, couldn't see that they were just little specks in God's great picture of my life. I tried to hold all these things lightly, even though, at the same time, I was grieving my loss. Loss of dear friends who were on the other side of the world; loss of my health, both mental and physical; loss of my ministry that had all dried up; and my identity – who was I now that I was back? If not a missionary, not a teacher, not a language student, then what? Drought had struck.

In my diary, I drew a picture of a solitary figure in the desert with a large sun overhead and wrote, *'Where in the desert am I? I might be a few sand dunes from the end. I might be near the start.'* Feeling stuck in the desert and weak, I gave up the job I had in a chocolate shop to spend the summer in a friend's empty house in the nearby countryside.

Chapter 17

Deep Roots in the Desert

沙漠之根

In Northern China there are severe water shortages as the desert steadily encroaches upon the cities, eating up the green earth and covering once-arable land with yellow dust and sand. To the North-West lies the vast and arid Gobi Desert, where at night the sky comes alive with thousands of sharp, cold stars, and for centuries the caravans and camels of traders passed under this sparkling canopy, treading for miles through the desert's long and inhospitable terrain, following the Silk Road to the West. The desert is ancient yet strong with age and not crippled; it slowly overpowers everything it touches. In my city, winds from the desert sometimes coloured the sky a dirty yellow during sandstorms, darkening the city and making it feel like the world was burning. The desert encroached on my heart and mind too. I began to have an insatiable desire to visit the desert, but the closest I ever got to the Gobi was in Katy's home county, where the bright blue sky strokes the orange earth and even the people's faces seem to glow red, their eyes perpetually squinting under a big, bold sun.

One afternoon in China, I dreamt about the desert. In the dream, I was walking through a field, then the field became a desert. I stood still, looking back over my shoulder at the way I had come through the desert. Perhaps I was on the edge of the desert, at its very end, but it was hard to tell because I was looking backwards, not forwards. The sky was blue and low, and the sand rolled away as far as my eye could see; it looked soft and yet it rose in steep and soaring dunes. Next to me stood a man. I was aware of his presence, though I did not look at him. He said to me, *"Were you afraid that you would get lost?"* I answered him, *"Yes, I was afraid because I didn't know where it would end. But it was beautiful."*

When I went to a friend's house in July 2017, a summer unusually hot and dry, the desert was again on my heart, because I felt more than ever like I was in one. But even the desert must have an end, I thought. During that time, I read the stories of Elijah and Elisha avidly. Elijah's drought ended eventually. The rain came, and plenty of it. And during those desert wanderings, God provided for Elijah and met with him in new ways, on deeper levels. These were two men who knew both the desert and the God of the desert well.

At this time, I was very low – physically weak and emotionally drained. Even a close friend coming to visit me for a cup of tea on a hot afternoon made me anxious. I felt like a mess, desperate and distraught, and I didn't know how to get out. I'd tried everything, and nothing worked. I was at the end of myself, 'hedged in,' stranded; my ways were blocked. I was also stranded quite literally in a small village in the middle of nowhere without a car or any public transport.

Then, after weeks of hot weather, it rained. It rained so heavily that it sounded like stones were falling on the kitchen roof. Streams of water fell to the earth. The fields outside the window were drenched, and from the cracked flower beds and parched cottage garden rose a wonderful rich smell as the earth drank deeply of the long-awaited rain. That afternoon I sat at the kitchen table and wrote a poem:

The Rain Will Come

I had been waiting days for rain
And then today it came
The clouds above they seemed to swell
Unable to contain

Such treasure stored within
Such unexhausted grace
And so they broke, the blessing fell
Upon my upturned face.

Before I walked on parched ground
Where dry and withered roots abound
Hoped I – the desert has an end –
And such an end that can be found!
God – He heard my secret whisperings
Saw me faint upon the sand
Waited only then to rend
Those hidden clouds, to drench the land.

Those little clouds as small as hands
Will soon become thick, dark bands
As rain in all its abundance falls
That deepest drought cannot withstand.
Go up, then, to the mountain, pray,
Though His promise tarries, it never delays
Safe is the wilderness where God calls
His children out, to test their faith.

Lilias Trotter wrote: *'The desert is lovely in its restfulness – the great brooding stillness over and through everything is so full of God. One does not wonder that He used to take His people out into the wilderness to teach them.*'[16] There was plenty of stillness in my desert, and a keen sense of aloneness. Most of the time I struggled to be there, considering it as anything but lovely, feeling only the heat and the weariness of desert wandering, seeing the wilderness only as a place of blighted trees and stunted shrubs; a God-forsaken place, vast and terrible. And yet God was present, even in a wilderness. And what seemed broken and in pieces, God was making into something new. To be truly alone with God in an

---

16 http://liliastrotter.com/quotes/

exposed place where there is nowhere to hide might sound frightening, but is actually the safest place to be.

After that summer, I went back to work in a shop, selling trashy crime novels and cheap stationery. After a while, I felt keenly the drudgery of working there and also, with self-pity, found myself thinking, *'I worked hard through University, I worked hard teaching, and I worked hard learning Chinese... what of all that now?! I don't need any of it to sell books!'* God's Word answered: *'God is the Judge; He puts down one and exalts another' (Ps 75.5)*, and *'God can be trusted not to allow you to suffer any temptation beyond your powers of endurance. He will see to it that every temptation has a way out, so that it will never be impossible for you to bear it' (1 Corinthians 10:13, Phillips)*. The way out, I realised, wasn't always a means of escape but rather a way to enable you to endure and continue to go on in whatever difficult circumstances you find yourself in. It was hard not to stop on the edge of all God's promises to me instead of continuing, believing that He would be faithful to His call and do what He had said. I was just to do the next right thing, leaving with God what only God could do, and though my heart felt battered and bruised and broken, I hoped that like spices that release their aroma when crushed, the weight bearing down upon me might also release something beautiful and fragrant in my life too.

On a busy train to London, where the aisles smelt like warm sandwiches and the air was perpetually punctuated by the scrunching sound of crisp packets, I overheard two old ladies discussing Isaiah 40 together. Intrigued, I opened my Bible. The chapter expresses God's tender heart towards His suffering people; He speaks comfort to them and tells them that their time of suffering and difficulty is over – God Himself is coming to their desert. God also challenges the complaints and doubting thoughts of those waiting for His deliverance:

'Why, O Jacob, do you say and declare, O Israel, my way and my lot are hidden from the Lord, and my right is passed over without regard from my God?

Have you not known? Have you not heard? The everlasting God, the Lord, the Creator of the ends of the earth, does not faint nor grow weary, there is no searching of His understanding. He gives power to the faint and weary, and to him who has no might He increases strength.

Even youths shall faint and be weary, and young men shall feebly stumble and fall exhausted; but those who wait for the Lord [who expect, look for and hope in Him] shall change and renew their strength and power, they shall lift their wings and mount up as eagles; they shall run and not be weary, they shall walk and not become faint or become tired' (verses 27-31, AMP).

There was me, thinking God had passed me over, thinking my life had been hijacked by illness, and I was to be forever stuck in this place of difficulty, trudging through a heartless desert. But God brought comfort to me on a stuffy, noisy train hurtling through the grey countryside, and I had courage yet again to go on, little by little, step by step, for all those littles and all those steps will one day make a great whole and become a long way.

Chapter 18

Return

归来

The first thing I noticed when I returned was just how dirty everything was. I'd never noticed it in quite the same way before. The sky, the ground, the buildings, the floor. Everything else seemed the same. The same expressionless customs officer who prised off my fingerprints with his blue machine and mechanically nodded me through the glass door; the same smell of compressed heat, steamed buns, and hot plastic that hit me when I stepped out of the plane door, the same old Chinese auntie running her mop over my feet in the Ladies on the way out of the airport. I had butterflies in my stomach while I waited in the queue for the baggage scanner, and I even allowed a large party of middle-aged Chinese to push in front of me while I stood on tiptoes trying to catch a glimpse of my Chinese flatmate through the glass panels into arrivals. In the faded BYD taxi, I peered out, through a smattering of rain, at the scenery rushing past us – the huge grey skeletons of high-rise buildings that stood like silent sentries along the highway. As we neared the city, I could make out once familiar landmarks that told me where we were in relation to our flat – the square yellow building that might have been a shopping mall; the TV tower, its top lost in clouds and smoke; the blue bridge spanning the road – until we turned into our small road lined with trees, silver and dusty with trunks painted white. When we got out of the taxi, we were opposite the rusty iron side gate to our complex, and the same old skinny uncles with missing teeth were playing Chinese chess with the same old aunties in their baggy flannel trousers at wobbly wooden tables perched on the uneven pavement. The feeling was odd. Even odder when I turned and bumped into an American mum with her two girls, and the conversation that followed was like I had never been away, like the last time I'd seen her was only yesterday. With a grey, overcast sky and dirty puddles on the floor, we wheeled my case through Rubbish Lane, dodging most of its sticky debris, and then pulled it up five flights of stairs to our flat door. Inside our flat, all was quiet. We sat on the faded leopard print sofa, its broken arms hidden under faded leopard print cushions, and ate chocolates that had melted and re-solidified many times, the bright red, orange, and green wrappers sticking to the chocolate so that we periodically had to pull bits of tin foil out of our mouths. I was back in China.

I rediscovered my life in China. I opened cupboards and found bundles of letters from students and friends and four years' worth of notebooks full of my scribbles. At four in the morning, succumbing to jet lag, I unpacked boxes covered in two years of dust and rediscovered the clothes I used to wear. It was like finding myself again. I spent the first day cleaning the kitchen, scrubbing away at its surfaces coated in thick layers of orange cooking oil, and making several trips downstairs to the convenience store to buy cloths, rubber gloves, and bleach. All the contents of the kitchen cupboards ended up in the outside bins and were salvaged triumphantly by old Chinese neighbours.

Walking the streets again, alone, I was strangely nervous of bumping into people I knew. Perhaps I was afraid of what people would say when they saw me. I looked a bit like a scarecrow – skinny with my hair cropped short and sticking up in the heat. After cleaning, food was my next priority. On the way to the supermarket, a good twenty minutes' walk, a small, lithe girl sprang off a bus and made a beeline for me. It was an old friend, and we spent the next day talking for six hours in the shady part of a café, sipping milk tea, with the windows thrown open to the hot dampness outside and the air below our knees buzzing with a succession of hungry mosquitoes. We walked through the green and shady campus of a nearby university, enjoying the rich, earthy scent of rain on dry soil, past red pagodas and silvery stone stools that stood rooted in the thick green grass. There was so much to talk about, and every conversation I had with friends that summer seemed to be as deep as the roots of the Wutong trees of that university and as rich as the waters that flowed from the cracked rock in front of the old library.

Eventually, the flat started to look more decent as two years of grime were wiped away. Slowly, long-forgotten words emerged from the inner recesses of my mind and rolled off my tongue like small, round Chinese acrobats, and gradually, relationships were renewed and re-established. When Anita discovered I was in China, she insisted we meet up together and visit Lucas in the Adult Welfare Centre (AWC), where he still lived. The following week, she took me to the tiny room she lived in, hidden away in an old, grey Soviet-style complex full of dark corners and doors that gaped like hungry mouths. Her room was neat and tidy – a small square with a bed, a keyboard, and a tiny electric stove on which she made rice porridge. It was another hot day, this one without rain, and Anita tried to feed me overripe peaches from a stash she had in her room. She took out a box of jewellery she had made with the orphans and insisted on pushing an orange beaded bracelet up my arm. When it was time to go, we took the bus out into the suburbs, passing villages, fields, and dried-up rivers, rumbling along with only the faintest of breezes from the open windows; the sky a brilliant blue above us and empty of even a wisp of cloud. The AWC was just the same. The mountain hadn't moved. Inside the compound, all was quiet. It was just after noon, and the roads were empty. We walked through the compound to the same small room we used to use, passing the washing lines where blue and white checked sheets hung stiffly above dust and sand and small patches of spikey grass that defiantly continued to grow despite the lack of water and the fierceness of the sun. We were soaked in sweat from the bus ride, and the small room was even worse than the metal bus, without air conditioning or windows that could open. Two fans on the ceiling hummed and pushed the hot air around the room. A few people were sitting inside, waiting for Anita, and others slowly emerged like shadows from the silent floors and soundless buildings around us. Some were mute; others were deaf or deformed; and some just looked worn-out and frayed around the edges. When Lucas arrived, he appeared unchanged. He had the same huge grin from ear to ear. He was still small for his age and thin. His hair, perhaps, was different, cut more fashionably, and there were the faint beginnings of whiskers on his face. But there *was* something different about him. *"I've grown up,"* he said in Chinese, and grown up he had. We tried to find a shady spot outside and ended up sitting on stone benches beneath overhanging greenery in the car park. Lucas had no idea that I hadn't been in China during the past two years. He'd been to a boarding school in a nearby city, learning computing. He told me about his plans to find a job in a computer company when he graduated, in a big city like Guangzhou or Shanghai. A man who worked in the AWC passed us on the way to his car and laughed. He asked me if I understood Lucas, talking over him in Chinese, and told me the school he was attending was for 'special kids.' He then moved away, still laughing. Lucas told me about his mother, who abandoned him at the age of five, and his hopes of finding her again. He told me about all the people upstairs who didn't come down. Then he went to wake Daniel I could say hello. Daniel used to be one of the Warrior children but had been sent back to the AWC because of challenging behaviour. When Daniel came down, he stood in the half-light of the corridor, blinking and half-dazed. I remembered that day long ago when I lost him in the park. When I gave him a bag of sweets, he put his hands together and bowed slightly before being escorted back to the elevator and up to his room somewhere higher up in the building.

When I arrived home later that evening, after a bowl of pumpkin porridge with Anita in a crowded corner of the city, I felt lacking. The day had been busy, and the volunteers who had joined us at the AWC had filled the afternoon with many activities. On returning, one had posted a comment on social media, sweet and kind, but referring to the people at the AWC as *'children.'* In some ways, they were like children – simple, limited by physical or mental disability, with limited education too. But many of them were older than me – older than this volunteer. I couldn't help thinking that they deserved respect and dignity and something more than dancing and craft – perhaps friendship and connection. Though activities may bring joy and a sense of purpose to hours otherwise unoccupied, the real needs of these people were the same needs that Lucas expressed when I sat with him under the sparse overhanging vines. The need to be seen and heard, made visible and safe in the presence of another person, emotionally held. I felt challenged.

I saw Lucas again. When I asked him if he was happy, he stoically replied, *"Life has happiness and it has sadness; happiness doesn't last forever."* Returning to the AWC, I took a lift with another volunteer. In her swish, air-conditioned car, she glided in and out of traffic, stopping to pick up another volunteer, a young man in beige trousers and a lilac shirt. These volunteers were successful, comfortable, and well-off, and yet they gave up their Saturdays to sit on blue plastic stools, silently perspiring, amongst friends at the AWC, simply chatting. When we left, we were escorted to the car by a group of people, who then pressed a large bag of walnuts into the hands of these volunteers. The female volunteer later wrote on social media: *'Because of work, I haven't visited you for some time. But you still remembered to pick walnuts for me. These are the best walnuts I've eaten this summer.'* Her comments and the way the people at the AWC treated her spoke volumes. And these volunteers weren't even Christians. Perhaps, as Christians, we are sometimes too good at doing things, putting on activities, and organising our 'works of compassion,' forgetting the simplest and yet hardest of things: just being with people and opening ourselves to them.

During those hot summer days back in China, I reconnected with old friends, some of whom I knew very well and others hardly at all. I was astonished to discover that many of my friends and acquaintances themselves suffered from colitis or knew people who did. It seemed in China that this disease was very common, and I was told by Zhao Yi (that Chinese man who used to pop up everywhere and popped up again on my plane home) that it was *'normal'* and *'not so serious.'*

I decided to go to one of the Children's Welfare Centres to see a small girl called Man Man, whom I used to look after. I ended up going every week and doing craft with the children, using up my large hoard of craft materials that I'd carefully accumulated over four years. Our sessions were noisy, chaotic, and messy, partly due to the inconsistency of the volunteers involved. There were new volunteers almost every week who were asked to teach or run an activity without knowing what the children were like or even how many there were. Management of these classes was sometimes difficult too. A slightly older boy of about nine or ten, took it into his own hands to 'discipline' the younger children who could not sit still. He hit them, pinched them, and threw them quite forcefully back into their chairs. This same boy took great interest in drawing a vase of flowers and asking me for more stickers as he sat quietly at his desk.

I sometimes felt disappointed in the Welfare Centre staff, who at times appeared disinterested in the children and were sometimes unkind. But then, there was much I didn't know. The child who asked me to undo the material that bound him to his wheelchair because it hurt him may have had good medical reasons to be tied in such a way. I hoped I would always have compassion. The next time I was able to interact with the stony-faced ladies who stood at the back of my class, I found them warmer than I imagined. I realised that it was easy for me to judge without fully understanding, easy to critique and spot gaps that needed filling, and easy to forget that the workers were only human with families and responsibilities, probably overworked and under pressure. There is perhaps often an underlying and hidden pride in being a Westerner in a developing country, of thinking we have got it all right. I realised then that during my time living in China, I had assumed I ought to meet the needs of all those I came into contact with. I had often taken on the role of *'rescuer,'* a role I could not fulfil and was not meant to. I had been so drawn into this mentality that I could not see that I had needs of my own. Indeed, when a young American woman I did not know well told me years earlier that she planned to burn out for God in China, I was secretly impressed, believing this was a noble thing! To me, the collapse I later experienced, was anything but noble.

It wasn't until my last week in China that I actually got a chance to see Man Man. Anita took me to an office in the Welfare Centre, and a lady with perfect posture and immaculate clothing escorted us across the grass to the building where Man Man was housed. Man Man's classroom was on the ground floor, at the end of a corridor. The lady went in and issued some short, sharp commands, and Man Man was led out to meet us in the corridor. The other children peered out at us from the windows. Man Man was thin, her legs were like matchsticks. Of course, she didn't know me. I held her and cuddled her on the cold, stone floor, and when she laughed, her laugh was like a flock of birds. But the smell from her mouth was over-powering; caught off guard, it nearly made me gag. Her teeth were all yellow, brown, and rotten. I had fifteen minutes with Man Man. When it was time to go, I slipped a yellow duck hairclip into her hair and handed her back to her carers through the door like she was a small, strange animal.

That summer, I was invited to an English Corner run by some of the volunteers that went to the Welfare Centres. It turned out to be a clandestine Bible study. We sat in a small office, on old sofas and fold-away chairs, halfway up an apartment block. We were a motley crew of Chinese and foreigner, with old Chinese aunties, young workers, and university students. The teaching was simple, but the discussions that followed were profound, and that small, messy room felt filled with the presence of God. At the end of the meeting, the foreigners were asked to share something with the rest of the group. When it was my turn, I started to share my story—the story that I have written in this book. I was surprised at how easily it flowed out of me, how the words came together perfectly, and how the people in the room listened intently. Most of these people were strangers, but in those minutes of vulnerability, of pouring out my heart before them, an intimacy was formed. It was humbling and yet it was also liberating, and I felt strangely empowered knowing that my story – or rather, God's story that He was writing in my life – was not meaningless and was not a story of failure, although it was a story of confusion, heartache, and difficulties. Yet, perhaps for the first time, I didn't just hope; but I knew for certain that God was doing something beyond me and above all I could hope or imagine. When I had finished telling my story to this group of strangers, taking far longer than the five minutes allotted me, the love they showered upon me, as someone closed in prayer, and then different ones came to speak to me, was what I can only use a Chinese phrase to describe: *an wei de* 安慰的 'comforting.' *An* 安 which means 'peace' or 'safety' is literally a picture of a woman sheltered, and *wei* 慰 which can be translated as 'to reassure,' is made up of heart, inch, and death. A heart that has known the death of something much loved is only ever an inch away from God and His comfort.

Chapter 19

Yin and Yang: At a Chinese Hospital
阴阳: 在中医药院

At the English Corner I met Abbie, a Chinese girl in her late twenties with a short bob and fresh face. She was soft, placid, and compared to my highly sensitive and emotional personality, half-asleep. After hearing my story and asking further questions about my illness, she told me (and several others listening into the conversation) that she was certain Traditional Chinese Medicine (TCM) could help me. She had trained as an acupuncturist and practised daily on herself for a stiff neck, achy back, and a dodgy stomach. She also happened to be living near me, so we walked home together after that first English Corner, under a hot sky that crackled with lightning and shook with thunder. She wasn't the chattiest, so our words soon became lost in our thoughts as we walked past groups of men laughing and joking as they sat on plastic chairs around plastic tables, their round stomachs poking out of rolled up T-shirts, skin glistening under lamps, and sweat pouring down their foreheads as they ate barbequed pork and squid and drank copious amounts of beer. Abbie was preparing for IELTS (an English language test that is required for studying at Western Universities) and had given up her job so that she could practise exam papers every day in the hope of passing and going to a Western country to continue her studies and bring Traditional Chinese Medicine to foreign countries. As I got to know Abbie and spent time with her, I came to realise two things: firstly, that her English wasn't good enough for her to pass IELTS, and secondly, that she desperately wanted to escape China. She had little love for her own people and her own nation and was both frustrated with and critical of modern Chinese society and, more dangerously, the Chinese government. She'd had a few wonderful encounters with generous and kind Westerners in Singapore and Malaysia, which seemed to have given her a rose-tinted view of Westerners and an insatiable desire to flee China and find freedom in the West. She had also recently become a Christian after her sister had accepted Christ into her life.

Late one night, Abbie messaged me and told me that she had a friend who was a TCM doctor, and he was willing to see me. I declined and told her my excuses (and genuine worries): it would cost too much, the needles might be unclean, it wasn't for me, a Westerner. The last is a genuine Chinese argument. Chinese often think that Asian things aren't suitable for Westerners because their bodies are somehow different. This includes eating spicy food, the climate, and Chinese medicine. Abbie seemed to accept these, and I thought that I wouldn't hear from her again on that subject. Then, about a week later, when I had nothing planned, Abbie messaged me and told me that the doctor would see me that very afternoon and that the consultation and any subsequent treatment would be free. Without anything else to do and unable to think of an excuse, I went.

The Provincial TCM Hospital's acupuncture department was situated in an old building, just a block from the bustling city centre. From the outside, it looked like it had seen better days and was hence very 'Chinese.' The yellow painted walls were stained brown in places, and large black smears ran down them. The outside units of air conditioners hung precariously to the walls and looked like their crumpled metal shells might at any moment let go of their grasp and land on the unsuspecting heads of pedestrians that ambled past the hospital seven stories down on the pavement. The main entry to this building was up some grubby stone steps, through dusty PVC curtains, and into a lobby. We shared the elevator to the seventh floor with several old Chinese people who spluttered and coughed and were attached to drips, and a nurse with a trolley full of large black bin bags. On the seventh floor, the lift doors opened to a corridor full of thick, white smoke, its fumes curling upwards and hovering over our heads in a dense cloud that covered us with a smell reminiscent of marijuana. We found Abbie's friend in a room halfway down the corridor, which was both the doctors' shared open plan office and their consultation room. Nothing in China is ever private, including going to see the doctor. Ricky Hu, the doctor, was tall and thin, wearing jeans that were cut too short, exposing a pair of knobbly, white ankles. He wore a white coat, out of which protruded a large head with a mop of messy brown hair. He reminded me of a big dog, the lanky type with a huge seal-like head, or an egg on the top of a pair of chopsticks. Ricky asked Abbie lots of questions about me, some of which I started to answer myself, as Abbie didn't seem to think it important to ask me these herself in English. He felt my pulse and peered at my tongue. He surprised me with some of his statements concerning my health and, unlike a Western doctor, seemed to have a more comprehensive understanding of my body. He said I was someone who couldn't tolerate the cold, who often had lower back pain, had difficulty sleeping, and got anxious easily. How he knew this just from listening to my pulse and looking at my tongue, I'll never know. He then took me and Abbie to one of the treatment rooms further up the corridor. There were three beds in the room (one already occupied by a middle-aged lady) covered by the most Spartan of white hospital bedcovers, slightly frayed and stained in several places. Ricky Hu, in his unhurried, nonchalant way, prodded my stomach, exclaimed *"Distension!"* in Chinese, and left us alone, returning to the room a few minutes later with several packets of needles. Using his teeth, he tore open the packets and, with his thumb, inserted the needles into my head, scalp, arms, wrists, stomach, and legs, each insertion extracting an *"Ow"* from myself, to which Ricky Hu only grinned and continued to puncture my skin. When he was finished, I couldn't move, as if impaled upon the hard bed. It hurt even to laugh. Ricky Hu had covered my body in at least thirty needles; I even heard Abbie exclaim, *"Name duo!"* 那么多 'So many!' I thought the worst of this torture was over when Ricky stuck his head out the door and called out to a nurse. She wheeled an archaic metal fan into the room. I felt hopeful; a nice breeze wouldn't have gone amiss in that stuffy, warm room, where tendrils of smoke were already creeping under the door from the corridor outside. Ricky rummaged beneath a bed and pulled out a power pack with wires sticking out of it. It reminded me of secondary school physics lessons, building circuits from wires and power packs. Unable to even raise my head slightly, bristling as I was with two-inch-long needles, I had no ability to object as Ricky fixed up the wires to needles on various points of my body (the meridian) and sent electric currents through them. This made the needles jump up and down on my belly in a strange, mesmerising dance. The metal fan unfortunately turned out to be the very opposite – a heat lamp – and was placed over my stomach as a sort of guardian to the whole process. I lay there half-paralysed and slightly nervous that the lamp, with all the feet that kept moving around that small room (Ricky's, the nurse's, Abbie's), might topple over on top of me and burn my stomach with a grill-shaped tattoo.

I was left in that uncomfortable state for over an hour. Abbie took several turns around the small room, and the middle-aged lady laughed from her bed with incredulity at being in a hospital room with a Westerner in the middle of China. After that first day of treatment, Ricky Hu asked me to come back the next afternoon. He suggested about nine rounds of acupuncture would be beneficial, and so, having started, I went back.

Ricky Hu's diagnosis was *'Spleen and Kidney Yang deficiency,'* which basically meant cold had set in and my inner fires had dampened. This was characterised by fatigue, loose stools, distention after eating, hair thinning, and lower back pain. One afternoon, when we went to the TCM hospital, we couldn't find Ricky anywhere. That afternoon, the corridor was even more smoke-infested than usual. We wandered around, peering into different rooms, coughing and flapping at the fumes with our hands, when, peeking into a particularly densely smoke-filled room, a dark head popped up from one of the beds and greeted us. It was Ricky, lying on his stomach in a room with four other men in similar positions. Each man was covered in a yellow piece of material, thicker than paper, and on the material were placed large pyramids of a dry, fluffy herb, stacked high, aflame, and slowly smouldering. Curls of white, musky smoke stung our eyes as we blinked and tried to make out Ricky's slender frame through the mist. It was somewhat reassuring to find a doctor, on a quiet afternoon, undergoing the same treatment that he daily performed on others. Abbie filled me in on this treatment. It's called moxibustion in English, *ai jiu* 艾灸 in Chinese, and the dry herb that is burnt is known as mugwort or wormwood. Moxibustion helps to heat certain areas, stimulating circulation, and can be used together with acupuncture to treat yang deficiencies. It wasn't long after this incident that Ricky Hu suggested doing it to me. Intrigued, I agreed. The next time we went to the hospital, Ricky asked us to bring salt and root ginger. The ginger he cut up into thick slices. Ricky poured salt into my belly button as I laughed, telling me to hold still because my laughter made the salt run down both sides. He placed a slice of ginger on top and then undid a moxa cigar, pulling out the dried herb and, using his finger and his thumb, pressing it into cone-shaped piles. These tiny pyramids sat upon the ginger and were then lit. When they burnt down, a new pile was placed on the ginger and lit again, so that the whole process took about an hour. After each pyramid, the ginger was hotter, and ginger juice ran down my stomach, leaving sweet, yellow streaks. The salt, too, began to melt. Ricky, on looking at the melted salt and trying to pull it out of my belly button with his little finger, appeared surprised and told Abbie it was evidence that I had too much dampness in my body. Ricky later taught me how to do moxibustion at home, and Abbie gave me a box of moxa cigars. My flat began to smell like a TCM shop. The water delivery man, whose delivery coincided with one of these moxibustion sessions, was amazed to find a foreigner practising *ai jiu* 艾灸 on herself. Unfortunately, although the application of heat was somewhat comforting and the smell grew on me, the long and short of my experimentation with moxibustion was that nothing overwhelmingly positive seemed to come from it. So, I eventually gave it up.

During my time fraternising with TCM, Ricky came up with a diet for me too. I told him about the Low FODMAP diet that my consultant had put me on in the UK, and which seemed to work reasonably well. Any deviation from that diet brought on symptoms, so I stuck to it quite rigidly, even in China, with temptation calling to me from every street corner and every steamed bun hole in the wall. Ricky's dietary recommendations were as follows:

1. 食物新鲜卫生.
   Food fresh and hygienic.

2. 养成良好的饮食习惯，营养均衡，规律饮食，细嚼慢咽。
   Cultivate a good habit of eating and drinking, balanced nutrition, a disciplined diet, eat slowly.

3. 食物宜用精米，精面粉，鸡蛋，瘦猪肉，牛肉，猪肚，鱼虾等。
   Diet should include refined rice, refined flour, eggs, lean pork, beef, pork belly, fish, shrimp, etc.

4. 禁食刺激性食品，如辛辣刺激等食物，如葱姜蒜，辣椒，麻辣火锅，酒水，芥末，咖啡等。
   Abstain from pungent/irritating food, such as hot spicy food, onion, ginger, garlic, chilli, spicy hot pot, alcohol, mustard, coffee, etc.

5. 忌食高纤维的蔬菜，水果；忌食坚果类，比如花生，瓜子，杏仁等，包括花生酱，芝麻酱等,油脂较多的食物。
   Avoid fruit and vegetables with high fibre, avoid all kinds of nuts, for example peanuts, sunflower seeds, almonds etc., including peanut butter, sesame paste etc., high fat/ oily foods.

6. 烹调以煮，烩，蒸等为主，不用油炸或浓调味品。炒菜放油不宜多。
   Cook mostly by boiling, braising, steaming, don't deep-fry or add lots of seasoning. Don't add too much oil to stir-fried dishes.

7. 腹泻禁食坚硬食物：如火腿，香肠，腌肉等。
   When you have diarrhoea avoid hard foods: ham, sausage, cured meat, etc.

8. 尽量避免生冷食品摄入，如冷饮，冰饮，凉菜，生鱼片等，避免从冰箱拿出的食物直接食物和饮用。
   As much as possible, refrain from raw foods, such as cold drinks, ice drinks, raw vegetables, raw fish etc. As much as possible refrain from food and drink taken directly from the fridge.

9. 还应注意，有人对牛奶（包括纯牛奶，酸奶等）肠道过敏可引起腹泻。所以慢性腹泻者通常了解自己哪些吃了之后会引起腹泻或使腹泻加重。凡曾经引起腹泻加重的食品应尽可能的避免。
   Also, in some people with oversensitive guts, milk (including pure milk and yoghurt) can cause diarrhoea. So, people with chronic diarrhoea should know what things cause it in themselves or make the diarrhoea worse. Avoid whatever previously made it worse.

To be honest, Ricky Hu's diet was quite similar to the Low FODMAP diet which he had poo-pooed, although the Low FODMAP diet was more specific and didn't limit my intake of nuts or prescribe me pork belly in particular. Ricky also taught me how to make a special porridge and encouraged me to make it every day. It consisted of black rice, millet, pearl barley, and an ingredient that I had to buy in a Chinese Medicine shop; Poria mushroom. I went to three different herbal medicine shops before I found Poria mushroom, and I was helped in the process by a kind, old Chinese gentleman. This man overheard me in the first shop asking for Poria mushroom, and guided me to the next shop. When they shrugged their shoulders, he took me outside and raised a gnarled finger to point down the road to the next herbal medicine shop. He asked me why I needed Poria mushroom, and when I told him my TCM doctor had prescribed it, he was frankly astonished and chortled heartily. *"Can a Westerner tolerate TCM?"* I was starting to wonder that too. Eventually, I found that magic mushroom. The herbal pharmacist shook white cubes onto his brass scales and then slid them into a brown paper bag and pressed it into my hand. This mushroom was hard, like a small cube of sugar, and had to be boiled for a very long time before it turned slightly softer and grey in colour. It was tasteless and the porridge was woody, so that an ample spoonful of brown sugar had to be added before the porridge was edible.

There was one hot afternoon I shared a room at the hospital with a Chinese family from one of the rural counties adjoining the city. They spoke with strong accents in a local dialect; their faces and skin were darker and swarthier and they wore leggings and polo necks, though it was the height of summer. Their mother, whom I mistook at first for a man (and was hence annoyed about the fact that he was in my room!) lay on the bed below the window. She was skeletally thin, with large ear lobes, whisks of white hair on her otherwise bald head, and was wearing a loose white T-shirt that exposed her thin, turtle-like neck. She lay in the bed, continually emitting a low groan that rumbled around the room. Her relatives sat on the spare bed, gossiping in an animated way and crunching sunflower seeds. When Ricky Hu came into the room to see me, the old lady called out to him. *"I'm dying, I'm dying, I'm dying,"* she croaked. Ricky stood over her and said, matter-of-factly, *"Bie shuo le"* 别说了 'stop talking,' or 'that's enough/let it rest.' The poor old lady continued to groan and call out in plaintive tones, *"I'm dying,"* long after he'd left. Her relatives ignored her until one, her daughter perhaps, hoisted her up and sat behind her, her knees forming arms and her body a chair for the old lady to lean back into. Then she gently rocked backwards and forwards, chanting *"e mi tuo fo"* 阿弥陀佛 'merciful Buddha!' I felt sad for this old lady, who was, as Ricky told us later, indeed dying. Her family could not give her any real hope, so that after the chanting was over, she continued to call out her cry of despair, and large tears rolled heavily down her cheeks. I asked Abbie if she could talk to the lady about Jesus in the local dialect or to her family, who had settled down into the spare bed and were now eating instant noodles, using their chopsticks to add emphasis to certain points in their conversation. But Abbie said they had their own religion; she couldn't tell them as it felt awkward and rude. So, all I could do was pray, being so close physically to these people, and yet so far away and unable to enter their world and show them the way. How sad to know that so many millions of Chinese are still without hope, without any knowledge of Jesus Christ the Lord, and

> *With none to heed their crying for life, and love, and light,*
> *Unnumbered souls are dying and pass into the night.*[17]

When I left that summer, I saw Ricky Hu a few days before leaving. I stopped by the hospital on my way somewhere else to say goodbye to Ricky. He wished me well and suggested a last bout of acupuncture, which I declined, and then he said everything would be much better when I was on my own *shui tu* 水土 'water and land'. That same old thing that surfaced everywhere – the fact that I was foreign. Abbie made it back from her own hometown to see me before I left. I gave her back her moxa cigars and thanked her for her care and all her trouble. She meant well; she wanted to help me, but it seemed like a long haul. I left both her, Ricky Hu, and all that I had experienced at the Chinese hospital feeling defeated and deflated. Everything about China was *man man* 慢慢 'slowly, slowly,' including Chinese medicine. Perhaps I was still hoping for a quick fix. I had taken Abbie's offer in hope, longing that it might be the Lord's Will for me and a way that would lead to that ultimate and complete healing that I was still holding out for. I had to be reminded that sometimes things take a very long time, even years.

---

17 Facing a Task Unfinished, a hymn by Frank Houghton

Chapter 20

The Chinese Landlord

中国的房东

My landlord was called Liu Peng, and Grace and I first met him in a tea shop to discuss the rental contract. That was June 2014, and we refused to drink hot tea on an already sweltering day, instead ordering cans of Sprite and perhaps thereby breaking a social norm. Ron, a very tall Chinese boy with eyes that crinkled behind metal frames when he smiled, and a special talent whereby he could tell a person's character from their smell, came with us and sipped the hot tea on our behalf. I had spent many afternoons sitting in cold noodle restaurants with Ron, looking at photos of potential flats on his laptop, and asking him to translate all the Chinese. Ron wrote everything down in his notebook meticulously and called all the numbers he'd carefully printed on the pages in a fine-nib black pen, asking all the questions I told him were important to a foreigner. Does it have two bedrooms? Air conditioning? A Western toilet? Prior to deciding to share a flat with Grace, I had been thinking of sharing with one of my students. We had been to a couple of different flats near my university campus and almost settled on one when I had second thoughts and pulled out. The landlady of that flat was a middle-aged teacher with thin lips and a permanent frown. One of the conditions of renting her flat was that she could leave all her stuff in it and her bedroom intact and untouched, so that she could periodically return home and spend the night there. My student didn't seem to think much of this, but I didn't want to be tiptoeing around this woman, squeezing my life into one cupboard in the kitchen and one of the two small bedrooms left for us. And then there was the prospect of dealing regularly with her mother, who came to all our meetings with her—a stern, older lady with tight curls and a wooden smile. So that summer, Ron accompanied me and Grace as we made several trips to view properties in a particular neighbourhood.

Thirty years ago, when it was probably very new, this neighbourhood had been a favourite place for expats to live due to the convenience of bus stops, and the fact that it was only a ten-minute walk to a main roadway. It was still a favourite place to live for a certain type of expat – the one who doesn't care about flashy new builds, frequenting bars, or only eating Western food in nice restaurants. The expats who lived in that faded part of town were either students who had to save their pennies, expats who had lived in China for donkey's years, their clothing style remaining firmly fixed at exactly the point when they left their homeland, or people who were in China for more significant reasons than just learning the language or teaching English, though they did both. Although there were quite a few expats living in the area, one hardly ever bumped into them, as we were always very much outnumbered by the Chinese. There was a park in the area that spanned two sides of a road, where the elderly congregated throughout the day – in the early hours to do Tai Chi, late morning to sing local opera, midday to nap in the shade, and in the evenings to take a stroll or join in square dancing. There were at least seven massage places, ranging from the walk-in foot massage clinics with doors that slid open onto the street, to the blind men's massage shop at the top of a set of narrow, dark stairs whose off-white walls were crumbling into small piles on the floor. There was a wet market where you could buy vegetables and fruit, meat and eggs, as well as different kinds of rice, spices, and noodles. There were a few restaurants, mostly small and grubby and therefore offering tastier food, and at night there were plenty of street vendors that appeared selling all sorts of street snacks, the air simmering with the smell of bubbling oil and hot chilli and with the sounds of voices laughing and chattering. It was a place that didn't look like much, but to those who ended up living there, it was special.

Before we met Liu Peng, we had visited a few questionable flats. In one, the shower hung over the squat toilet in a truly miniscule bathroom. I wondered how one could shower without falling in the toilet when the floor was wet, or if the toilet would overflow with all the wastewater from the shower? There was also a ground-floor flat with a bare stone floor and a wooden bed without any legs. Some of the windows were blocked up with old newspapers, and the lighting came from bare bulbs that flickered and buzzed. I was tempted to live in a cheap place in what I felt were quite authentic surroundings, showering over a toilet and sweeping a dirt floor, but I'm glad Grace won out and we found more comfortable digs. The one we settled on, Liu Peng's flat, was on the fifth floor of a squat building that had a poorly lit stairwell with windowless windows enclosed with bars. It was spacious inside, with a small kitchen that seemed to hang out over the small square below; a large living room, a small balcony, a large bedroom with air conditioning, a smaller bedroom without, and a bathroom in between, which had a glass panel in the door but no window looking outwards and therefore was both dark, dank, and infested with silverfish bugs. The furniture was an eclectic mix of very solid stuff, that was very difficult to move, with a lot of glass-topped surfaces that showed up dust very easily, and a number of items that were neither pristine nor modern. We decided on it very quickly, and with Ron's help, we signed Liu Peng's contract. Liu Peng appeared to be a very amiable landlord, slim and not unattractive, with a wife who taught English at my university and was a believer. Liu Peng was quite chatty, though he often turned up at unsociable hours to check on things or attempt to fix something and stayed for ages, unaware that we wanted to go to bed and his presence in our flat was preventing it. When something was broken, he always called up the same two plumbers, who must have lived nearby because they always showed up quite quickly, regardless that it might have been ten thirty at night. These men were dark-skinned, with wrinkled faces, wearing oily jackets soaked in cigarette smoke, and always hauling along a bag of old hammers. They never seemed to have the right tools, often asked for torches to peer into dark places, and one would always disappear for half an hour in search of some other equipment.

In China, things seem to break easily and often. Perhaps it's the dry air. Things became old quickly and sort of dry up. The first thing to go in our flat was our shower. It was working when we moved our stuff in that first summer, but in the space of six weeks of non-use, it grew despondent, felt unwanted, and gave up the ghost. Then there was the toilet, whose flush, for a long period of time, only gave out a trickle of water when pushed. We resorted to using buckets to flush until, months later, Liu Peng eventually sorted it out, and after that, it worked sporadically. The long tube light bulbs in the living room periodically shattered and fell down. Even my clothes horse broke, but that was because Liu Peng leaned on it in an offhand manner, running one hand through his hair, as he talked to me, and the thing cracked and part of it snapped off, causing Liu Peng to splay sideways.

When I arrived back that summer after two years away, I discovered several problems. The door handle had fallen off the inside of our front door, so every time we needed to close it, we had to slam it hard, pulling our fingers out of the way very quickly before they got chopped off. Closing and opening the door became a high-risk endeavour. However, the biggest problem was that every time we used the shower, our kitchen flooded. This had been fixed by those two swarthy plumbers, but after some time had passed, as was usually the case, the problem resurfaced. One evening, Liu Peng turned up to show some potential new tenants around the flat. He arrived at eight in the evening, just when I'd finished cooking my dinner, so that while I was slurping up spaghetti at the glass table in our living room, he was showing a family of Chinese around the flat. I smiled a tomatoey grin and waved at them. Unfortunately, I had left a tea towel on the kitchen floor to soak up the water from my shower, and the Chinese family noticed this and wondered whether it was a Western custom or if there was a problem with the plumbing. Liu Peng laughed it off – just a slight problem – and questioned me. I replied in Chinese *"showering water flows"* and pointed below the sink with a *"from there."* Liu Peng's grin fell at one corner, but in his always genial mood, he said it was a small thing and he would fix it immediately. When the family had left, and after a brother-in-law had turned up to have a look around and give his opinion, Liu Peng whipped out his mobile and called the two plumbers. They both had flat feet, so we heard their arrival, clomping heavily up the stairs, even before they knocked on the door. Liu Peng was on them in a shot. He beckoned them to the kitchen and waved his arms around in a very animated manner, and a late-night argument ensued, from which I detected, *"you fixed it!"* and *"my floor will be ruined!"* amongst all the shouting. The poor old plumbers grunted and scratched their heads, poked about under the sink, and hit some metal pipes with their hammers, with no consideration that their clanging and clanking about might disturb other residents in the block at ten at night. It turned out they didn't have the right tools with them, and although Liu Peng insisted that they return later that night to carry out the work, he seemed suddenly to remember that there were two of us who lived in the flat and might be more than a little peeved at the prospect, my flatmate having just returned home from work. *"Six in the morning, then,"* he said. I had a quick discussion with my flatmate, and she managed to convince Liu Peng that eight would be fine and her dad would come over too to help out in her absence. Unfortunately, things turned sour the next day, and Liu Peng and my flatmate's dad had a bit of a barney. Her dad left feeling insulted and spent numerous phone calls and conversations in the following weeks going over what was said between them and how it made him feel. Later still, when I had left again, Liu Peng refused to return most of the deposit, and so our seemingly easy-going landlord turned out, in this case, to be rather unpleasant after all.

Chapter 21

Wu Shi Ren Fei

物是人非

Going back to China that summer gave me that feeling of *Wu shi ren fei*: things have remained the same, but people have changed. My female friends had all blossomed into young ladies. The babies had all grown bigger. Male friends now had jobs and were successful. Many of my friends were now married, or on the verge of matrimony. And yet, despite the changes that time inevitably brings, connections were restored, strengthened, and deepened, so when I did finally leave, I once again left my heart behind.

Every time I went back to see the babies, I took something with me from my stash of playthings—puppets, bubbles, ribbon, and eventually even a Christmas tree. I recognised Xiao Bo immediately, though he had grown significantly and was no longer crawling but charging about the flat. And he had words. Not all of the aunties understood him all of the time, but that didn't stop words from rolling off his tongue, and they seemed to bounce up and down as much as he did. We reconnected almost instantly, though he probably couldn't remember me. We pretended his toys could fly, and he flew too, perched on top of his stuffed crocodile, waving down at the toys left behind. He loved being held up so he could point to the children in the photos on the wall and tell me their names. An auntie chided him for being in my arms and told him he was too big for cuddles. At four years old, he was the eldest child. Reluctantly, I put him down.

There was an afternoon when Xiao Bo, after eating his own lunch, attempted to eat some of the aunties.' He was smacked and placed promptly in the playpen where I was sitting. His tears resulted in further scolding from the aunties, now tucking into their lunch at the table, telling him he was too big to cry. The aunties ignored him, and after a while I held out my arms to him and he climbed into my lap, where he sat silently trembling. Another smaller child was sitting in front of us, moving bricks around the mat. After some time, Xiao Bo reached out an arm to swipe them. *"Don't hit,"* I said. *"Play with little brother and help him."* For the first time since I'd been there, the two children played together without hitting or fighting.

Star was still in the home too. Thin and unable to sit up unsupported, she spent most of the day lying on her back. She loved attention and would pull herself over to where I happened to be, even pulling herself over my legs or holding onto my toes. Her almond eyes were like the eyes of a deer. And Peter was there too, tottering about on his thin legs, running onto the balcony, and blinking in the light.

As the plane took me further away from China, I held all these things in my heart. And as Zhao Yi dozed in the seat beside me, I said goodbye to the loved ones I left behind once again in China.

I Left You Behind

I left you behind
On the Eastern side
Of the world.
I left behind me
Your silent sorrow
My sleepless nights
Waiting for the sky
To turn yellow.
I left behind me
Her almond eyes like the eyes of a deer

Her deep laughter like a flock of birds
His tears which I never saw him cry before
You said happiness isn't forever
有开心 有难过[18]
She said life is never easy
There must be someone who loves me.
I left behind me
Your face in my mirror
The roses dying on the table
That moment
We forgot
To guard
Our hearts
And let them spill.
I left behind me
Streets full of dust
Rooms full of voices
A sky full of God.

I felt like I had been there forever
But then I was gone.

---

18 There is happiness, there is sadness.

Chapter 22

The Ordinary Road

平凡之路

I returned to England with no major breakthrough in my health and no sudden opening for a return to China. Instead, I had cleared my flat, locked the door, and given the key back to my landlord. It felt like an end. Of course, I had harboured a secret hope in my heart – a hope that somehow I was still called to China, and that the *'crook in my lot'* that had forced my path in an entirely different direction to where I had wanted to go might yet be removed by God. I had applied my utmost force to make my crooked path straight, only to find my attempts were all in vain. Only God can make straight what He has made crooked, and only in His perfect timing.

At first, I felt a lightening of my heart, as if the burden I had been carrying for so long had finally been removed. Having left China with the words of many friends echoing in my ears, asking me to come back soon, and still convinced that God's promises would somehow someday be fulfilled, I was able at first to rest and put China aside for some time. Then came a fresh wave of grief. I felt that God couldn't have done a better job of breaking my heart so completely. As a consequence, I allowed myself to stand in the wind and be bashed about a little longer by it.

At that time, a certain Chinese song reflected some of my feelings and encapsulated some of my experiences. It is called *'The Ordinary Road:'*

Those who are hesitating on the road
Are you leaving now?
Being fragile and proud
That was how I once was.

Those who are passionate and restless
Where will you go?
Like a mystery, and so silent
Are you really listening to the story?

I've crossed mountains and oceans, and wandered through huge crowds
Everything I once had faded away in the blink of an eye.
I was once frustrated and disappointed, lost all direction,
Until I saw that the only answer was the ordinary road.

While you are still wondering
About your future
Will it be better or worse?
For me, it's just another day.

I once ruined everything, all I wanted was to leave forever.
I once fell into endless darkness, I struggled, but I couldn't free myself.
I used to be like you, like him, like that wild grass, those wild flowers
Full of despair, longing, and crying, smiling and being ordinary.

Move forward, just forward, no matter what you've been through.
Move forward, just forward, no matter what has been taken from you.
Move forward, just forward, no matter what you will miss.
Move forward, just forward, no matter what you…

I once asked the whole world, but never got an answer.
I used to be like you, like him, like the wild grass and flowers.
The only road I want to take is in darkness.

Time has no words, it just moves on.
Tomorrow is already in sight.
Where the wind blows the path stretches on.
Where is your story up to now?

That was me. Someone who had hesitated on the road for so long, stuck in one place. The only path that I was willing to take was not only in total darkness, but blocked by a huge boulder so that I could not go forward, even if I wished. I was fragile and proud, passionate and restless. At one point in time, it felt like everything that I had in China – my life, my friends, my ministry – had vanished like smoke, and I had been left disappointed and frustrated, so that I easily lost hope, lost heart, and lost sight of what life really means. There was a time when I despaired, a time when I struggled against God, and a time when I held all these things silently in my heart, unable to share them with anyone else but God. It was a never-ending cycle of despair, longing, crying, and then hoping again after He'd spoken. Maybe through this process He was healing me – not just physically but spiritually, emotionally, and mentally. I didn't know there were so many layers. I didn't know things went so very deep.

And then, just as the song says, I had to learn to live within the ordinary. My peace of heart came from learning to see God in all things, even the ordinariness of life, and knowing too that I had never been alone in this struggle. God had always been leading me. It may have felt like walking in the dark, but it was not. After the ocean depths come the ocean shallows, the way of small things. Living in the ordinary was the only way forward for me. I spent a long time looking down a path that was blocked and an even longer time looking back over my shoulder at the way I had come. But in the end, all I could do was move forward, to go ahead along the way that was open. Go forward, don't stay on the old road. Move ahead bravely, no matter what you've been through. He is leading you. Move ahead bravely, no matter what you feel has been 'taken' from you. God is no man's debtor. His way is always best. Go ahead bravely, even if that way feels like it lacks the richness of the way you have come. You will be surprised. He may take you to richer places yet.

Time rushes on. Another year has passed. Where is my story up to now? I'm still walking on an ordinary road, but I have a feeling in my heart that it may turn out to be extraordinary yet.

Chapter 23

A Plentiful Rain

降下沛雨

This book began in a small room that smelt like recently hoovered carpets, cooked dinners, and French-language textbooks. The large lady with bright hair teaching the creative writing course wrote several words on the white board and asked us to write down every thought that came into our heads in association with those words. My word was rain. All I could think of was China. Memories flowed out of my heart through my hand and onto the notebook in front of me. It was an outpouring. It was grief. It was some sort of painful love that I had held on to long enough and needed to release.

This was the autumn of 2017, a year after I had returned from China. And though sitting in that warm room every Wednesday afternoon for three hours made my stomach twist into a knot, my book began to form, fragmented at first, just bones, and then fleshed out, embodied. In China, I had no time to think or to feel, no space to process life with its ceaseless pace, but afterwards, in these years that seemed small and unpromising and unbearably empty, feelings, impressions, and images rose to the surface, and I scraped them off and put them into words.

Admittedly, this book was also an attempt to try to decipher what God was doing. In writing it, I hoped to see a pattern, some clues, a message that perhaps I had missed before, or anything else to make sense of it all. I wanted to know why things had gone wrong. Was it something I did?

Had *I* gone wrong? If only I could understand what God was doing, then, I thought, I could accept it because I would know its purpose. Instead, I was left with a story that didn't really give any answers at all. Yet through it all, I could see His Hand, His shaping of me as He pens my story, though the riddles and puzzles have not all been resolved or understood by me.

In China, I prayed a type of prayer that should come with a warning. It was one of those prayers that is an ache in a heart that longs for more of God and sees only its own shortcomings, its sad and sorry mistakes. God answered those prayers, but what a way! He answered those prayers by doing what I did not want Him to. He brought me back, and He took away what I held as more precious than anything else in my life.

But it didn't stop there. He was doing immeasurably more than I could ask or imagine, and though it seemed like He was constraining me, narrowing me, and bringing me to nothing, I think in actual fact He was enlarging me, reviving me, and restoring me by taking me beyond myself and into Himself.

I began working at a special needs school. Here, I learnt how to love what I thought was unlovable. It was another journey into a deeper place of trust. Very soon, I started to work with a young man who not only had special needs, but a history of neglect and abuse. He was always in an elevated state, easily tipping into fight or flight, hypervigilant, and therefore never feeling safe. I had no knowledge of anything that could help this boy. I was out of my depth, afraid of getting physically hurt, and unable to see anything good or lovely about him. Yet God commissioned me to work with him alone for hours every day. This was most definitely a lesson in learning to depend on God more fully, in living out the belief that whatever happens to me has first to pass Him by. If I was hurt, He must have allowed it, and if the very worst was to happen, then I knew there was good in it for me because it had to have come from Him.

Some of my colleagues, after being hurt and because we were, in the end, just low-paid, untrained people, were reluctant to work with this child. It somehow worked out that I spent a great deal of time with this young man. At times, I was overwhelmed. It was tempting to try to get out of having him so often, to go to management, or try to change the situation. But I was learning not to take things into my own hands, not to try and manipulate things for my own good. God saw me. He alone knows the motives of our hearts, and only God can vindicate His people, not themselves. Honour became a word I wanted to grasp and outlive. I began to pray the prayer of Jabez, a man who was described as *'more honourable than his brothers.'* Jabez prayed:

'Oh, that You would bless me and enlarge my border, and that Your hand might be with me, and that You would keep me from harm so that it might not bring me pain' (1 Chronicles 4.10, ESV).

I did get hurt. But not very much and never seriously. And as time passed, I developed a relationship with this traumatised young man. Through play, we connected, and trust was built. I began to see him. His favourite game was one in which an earthquake would suddenly strike his room, and he and his toys would end up squashed or trapped. I would call the rescue team, and they would come and rescue him (often a rather long-winded process). A massive celebration would follow, complete with camera crews and interviews. Through this play, I saw the heart of this boy. His world had been and was a world of chaos, in which he was injured and trapped, but always, through play, someone was coming to find him, to save him. We played out what he needed and wanted in his own life. And change, slow as it sometimes is, began to happen through the improvised and shared games of a young woman who desperately wanted herself to be saved, seen, and made safe in her own life too.

There is a patience that continues with what it is given to do, despite feelings and circumstances, while holding something greater and dearer in its heart. It is a power to continue despite what you may believe is stacked against you. God gave me strength to continue doing my duty, and in walking the simple, narrow path I found myself on with Him, I discovered some joy that went no small way to easing my own heartache. I found a real freedom and creativity, an unlocking and release of what I think is His life and goodness within me, when I was able to love and enjoy those who themselves bear tremendous difficulties and yet are always unreservedly and unashamedly themselves.

It seems to me that I discovered my heart for children with special needs in China, but that love was grown, stretched, and broadened here – tested even. Here in my own weakness, in my own struggles with illness and anxiety, and a thousand things I held that had no answers, God began the process of opening me up, shedding layers one at a time.

This is a God who rides through deserts, who marches through the wilderness. The heavens pour down rain at the presence of God. This is our God, who bears our burdens and carries us day by day, a God of deliverances; to Him belongs our escape from death, setting us free.

'You, O God, did send a plentiful rain; You did restore and confirm Your heritage when it languished and was weary' (Psalm 68.9).

To learn more or contact Joanna Gadd email

plentyofrain@yahoo.com

Inspired To Write A Book?

Contact

Maurice Wylie Media

Your Inspirational Christian Publisher

Based in Northern Ireland and distributing around the world.

www.MauriceWylieMedia.com

Maurice Wylie Media
As an appreciation of your order to receive 5% off use the following code
THANKINGYOU

9 781915 223272